The Author

MICHAEL F. ANDREWS received his Bachelor of Fine Arts in Art Education and his Master of Science in Art Education from the University of Kansas. He holds a Ph.D. in Fine Arts from Ohio State University.

He is co-author of *Growing With Art*, and editor and author of *Aesthetic Form and Education*, and *Creativity and Psychological Health*. His work appears frequently in educational journals.

As a sculptor, he has exhibited throughout the United States and received numerous awards.

Dr. Andrews is currently Dual Professor of Art and Education and Head of the Art Education Area at Syracuse University.

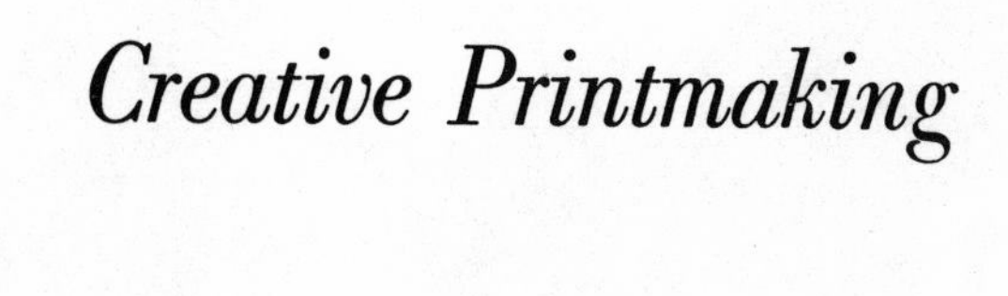
Creative Printmaking

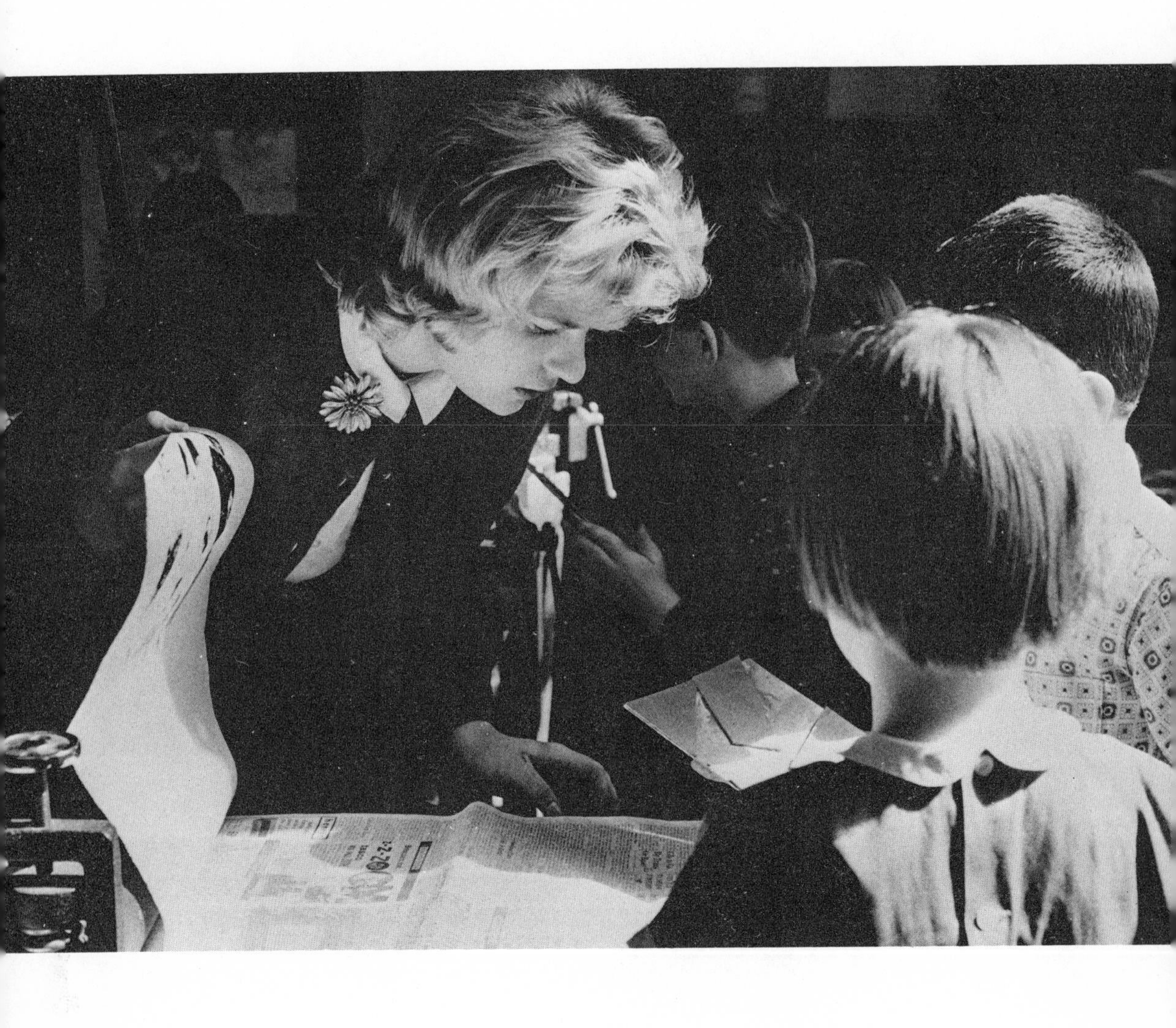

MICHAEL F. ANDREWS
Syracuse University

Creative Printmaking

. . . for school and camp programs

PRENTICE-HALL, INC., *Englewood Cliffs, New Jersey*

PRENTICE-HALL INTERNATIONAL, INC., LONDON
PRENTICE-HALL OF AUSTRALIA, PTY., LTD., SYDNEY
PRENTICE-HALL OF CANADA, LTD., TORONTO
PRENTICE-HALL OF INDIA (PRIVATE) LTD., NEW DELHI
PRENTICE-HALL OF JAPAN, INC., TOKYO

Current printing (last digit):
12 11 10 9 8 7 6 5 4

Library of Congress Catalog Card Number: 64–10501

Printed in the United States of America
C–19090

Preface

The art of printmaking is as old as art itself, and yet, only within the past decade or two has printmaking been recognized as a separate art, equal in importance and in creative potential to painting and sculpture. Originally, the artist used the printing process to make reproductions of his sketches. Although there are those who still consider the printing concept as merely an extension of drawing, printmaking is no longer a handmaiden; it is, instead, considered as one of the fine arts most peculiar and appropriate to our time.

Printmaking today is a popular art accepted by millions of people throughout the United States. This fact is manifest not only in the increasing number of printmakers, collectors, and print clubs, but also by the increasing amount of literature dealing with the subject, the inclusion of printmaking in the elementary and high school curricula, and the evident prominence of prints in local and national exhibitions. However, the necessity of a complex mechanical process, combined with the false assumption that expensive and cumbersome equipment is needed for this process, has prevented adequate teaching of printmaking in the field of art education. Nevertheless, there are indications that, with the innovation of a simple and concise technique, and with the use of inexpensive materials which lie within the capabilities of most venturesome amateurs, printmaking will find its place at all levels of education.

The public's active interest in the creative process has given vital nourishment to a great renaissance in printmaking. The advent of new materials and simple techniques and the feasibility of combining them have given us a greater potential for artistic expression. Printmaking is no longer neglected by the art teachers who are even remotely interested and concerned with a well-balanced art program. In the future, when we think of printmaking being taught in the schools, we will no longer think merely of a black and white impression of a Christmas symbol done on a small three-by-five-inch linoleum block. We will, instead, envision a colorful display of technical virtuosity which rivals the best of drawing and painting as an aesthetic expression.

The number of books dealing with the subject of printmaking is increasing. Unfortunately, many of them are far too technical and complex to be useful to elementary and high school teachers and students. Many of the books more suitable for public school and camp use are incomplete, making specific reference to only a few of the graphic techniques, omitting any discussion of the others.

The purpose of this book is to serve in a special way the needs of elementary, high school, and recreation art programs. It will do this, it is hoped, by introducing the wide range of possible experience in printmaking that is afforded by a variety of materials and techniques, and by providing the teachers and students with a background against which new ideas may be tried.

This book is, actually, a guide which concentrates largely upon the relatively simple techniques of the various printing processes and attempts to modify them so that they lie within the range of *all* school children. In a sense it is dually cumulative in character: it progresses from simple to more complex methods of printing; and from elementary relief on to the stencil, advancing into photographic and lithographic processes, and finally covering more complex intaglio methods of printing.

We trust that as the student becomes fascinated and ever more alert to the creative possibilities of his materials and techniques he will explore, experiment, and develop for himself his capacities of observation, judgment, and appreciation.

My profound gratitude goes to all my teachers: my father and mother whose understanding and creative guidance helped formulate my philosophy from the very beginning; the many children who shared with me their invaluable experiences; the artists, authors, and host of individuals who through controversy or consonance have contributed to my way of thinking; and the multitude of mystic forces which have influenced my life unbeknown to me.

I gratefully recognize my indebtedness to my wife Helen for her patience and moral support, and my son Mike and daughters Judi and Connee for the time they sacrificed that rightfully should have been theirs.

Especial acknowledgment is rendered to two of the most unforgettable teachers that I have had the pleasure and good fortune of studying with: Professors Maud Ellsworth and Erwin Frey. It was they who so generously gave their precious time and untiring effort and the wisdom which provided me with the incentive to ask, "Why seek the aesthetic life?"

I am indebted too to the following people for their cooperation in making this book possible: to Charles Giordano and Norman Williams, who gave me the necessary impetus to tackle such a project; to John Vargo for his assistance in laying out the book; to Henry W. Ray for sharing his creative ideas on experimental photography; to Fred Demarest for the aesthetic examples of photography which appear in the chapter on photography; and to the Art Institute of Chicago, the National Gallery of Art, and the Brooklyn Museum of Art for some of the prints that appear throughout these pages; to the children, college students, and professional artists whose art works appear within; to my secretaries, Cleone Libman and Ann Epstein, for diligently typing and retyping the manuscript; and to those whose faces so graciously adorn the pages of this book and whose names should be included but, due to the author's shortsightedness, are inadvertently omitted. Others are gratefully acknowledged throughout the text of this book.

M. F. A.

Contents

2

The Stencil Printing Process, 43

3

The Photographic Printing Process, 65

Creative Printmaking

Introduction

In spite of the fact that definitions are deadly instruments, it seems most desirable to indicate at least a point of view which will serve as a guide to creative printmaking. My only concern in attempting to define the process of printmaking is to establish some kind of standard by which we can structure future printing experiences. Printmaking has too often been defined as a relatively complicated process in which ink or paint is spread upon a prepared surface which in turn transfers an impression upon another surface by means of applied pressure. Unfortunately, printmaking thus defined makes reference only to the mechanics of reproduction. The principle of printmaking, however, has an even greater advantage than the mere reproduction of numerous prints from a single impression. Its greatest value lies in its function as a creative communications medium. Creative printmaking is thus actually comprised of two entirely different but inseparable disciplines. There is the aesthetic experience, on the one hand, and the technical approach to artistic production, on the other. These are integrated for the express purpose of communicating vital experiences. It takes both to produce a great work of art.

There is, however, a fundamental difference between the two. The first, the aesthetic, is the perpetuation of a harmonious relationship with one's environment—the struggle to be oneself, to seek basic truths, to objectify the innermost thoughts and feelings, in other words, to be creative. This involves the process of creative participation. Each individual must experience, in accordance with his intrinsic nature, the framing of purpose and the significance of expressing his own insights and interpretations. The creative process cannot be taught, it can be experienced only by means of self-participation. Since true values lie in a whole-hearted enlistment of the self in doing, there is relatively little that we as teachers can do in regard to this self-centered experience. If the student, however, is left to himself, without guidance, he is likely to remain at a low level of aesthetic development and the resultant prints will be incoherent and diffuse. Many more prints have been referred to as hackneyed because they said nothing than because they had something but did not know how to say it.

If we are concerned with permitting each student to find expression and the fulfillment of his own potentialities, we must stimulate his consciousness toward a structuring of reality by providing favorable conditions for the manifestation of his creative spirit. We must create an atmosphere in which the student can remain free, affording him the opportunity to experiment and explore, and to experience that which is unique and real, knowing that all sincere expression is worthy of respect.

The second component of creative printmaking is the technique through which ideas find expression. By itself, technique is no more art than grammar and rhetoric are literature. But matters of technique, especially those which include the investigation of everything that enters into the realization of creative ideas, are undoubtedly important. Technical dexterity represents the means of giving visual form to intellectual and emotional interpretations. Anyone who has experienced the creative process cannot help but recognize his dependence upon technical knowledge, especially if he is to realize his ideas in artistic forms. Students who have a richness of experience and a desire to express themselves must, of necessity, have the proper tools and technical skills to do so. Technical efficiency is the fundamental that underwrites the quality of all great art. It is important, however, that techniques be taught relative to the student's interest and at his level of development. Technical achievement, in its true form, is significantly a positive process. But when one's desire for creative expression is dominated by imposed disintegrative techniques, practiced in isolation, expressions remain inane and the technical process is a negative one.

There can be no abstract formula for the production of good art. Technical knowledge, which cannot be integrated, usually restricts the progress of creative thought and action. It is, therefore, imperative that techniques be developed, not taught. They must be born out of the need for self-expression. When properly developed, technical proficiency provides the student with a basis upon which more personal interpretations can be expressed, and permits him to enter into a whole new range of creative situations from which he was previously excluded. Technical proficiency does not ignore the personal equation. Its primary consequences, as a matter of fact, are found in the expression of personal strength and integrity.

Essential to the production of a good print are ideas stimulated by personal experiences and an appropriate technique to express them. Finding this integral balance between symbolic expression and disciplined craftsmanship is the everlasting obligation of every teacher during any printmaking project. Since the teacher who comes into direct contact with the student can best nurture his creative powers—and since overemphasizing aesthetic theory while omitting technical principles can lead to confusion about what makes a good print—the method of approach outlined in this book will primarily inculcate a conceptual and technical attitude toward printmaking.

There are five basic principles of printmaking: relief, stencil, photographic, planographic, and intaglio. With the exception of photography, all the methods involve the transfer of ink or paint to a surface in order to obtain an impression. Photography uses the medium of light. Although photography is not too well known as a printmaking process, it deserves mention for its simplicity and adaptability to photograms and cliché verre.

The five printmaking processes will be discussed as a series of separate methods in the order of their simplicity and popularity. These five basic types, for the most part, will be mentioned in their pure forms but they may be used as mixed media in combination with one another. The *relief printing process* is perhaps the simplest and most direct, and requires the least amount of equipment. The relief print is made from a raised surface that is inked, applied to another surface, and subjected to a certain degree of pressure. The *stencil printing process* is the newest of the printing media. The resultant print is made by forcing ink or paint through an opening in the stencil or, in the case of silk screen, through the perforations of the screen. Unlike the relief printing process, there is no reversal in the finished design. In the *photographic printing process* the impression is made on chemically sensitized paper with the aid of light. As in the stencil printing process, there is no reversal in the final print. The *planographic printing process* rivals relief printing as the most direct method. A planographic impression is made by drawing with a grease crayon or pencil upon a surface that has an affinity for both grease and water. Through the antagonism of grease and water, the impression is transferred onto another flat surface. The *intaglio printing process* is one of the oldest and most complex. The print is obtained from indentations that are cut or etched and lie below the surface of the printing plate. The ink is placed in the lower recesses of the plate and forced into contact with damped paper under a sufficient degree of applied pressure.

1

The Relief Printing Process

Of the five major printmaking processes, the relief or raised-surface method of printing is probably the oldest and, because of its simplicity, the most popular. Its origin is usually traced to early Chinese stone-rubbings of the second century. The principle of relief printing, however, can be found in the prehistoric cave art at Lascaux in the Dordogne and at Altamira in the north of Spain, dating from approximately 25,000 years before the Christian era. This type of printing may have been discovered accidentally since every man at one time or another has made impressions from smudged hands transferred to another surface. True printmaking on paper, nevertheless, did not come into existence in Western art until the middle of the twelfth century, years after the Western world had learned the secret of making paper. These first prints were in the form of woodcuts and wood engravings. Since then there have been many modifications and improvements in the techniques of relief printing. Today just about anything that will leave an impression on a material is used in printing.

With the innovation of better tools and techniques, and the discovery of many new materials, there has been a constant refinement in relief printing. Andrea Montegna, Hans Holbein, and Albrecht Dürer, during the high Renaissance, produced woodcuts and wood engravings that, in the dramatic impact of their light and dark areas, reveal force, power, and the intense feeling and imagination essential to a great print. The Japanese, at the beginning of the nineteenth century, were widely known for the simplicity of form in their bold, colorful prints. In the modern approach to printmaking, the Western artists are achieving a richness of color and a refinement of delicate lines resulting in a uniformity of tone, a display of technical integration and unity of feeling, and a degree of graphic expression that has never before been achieved.

More important than the technical changes that have occurred is the freedom that the students now enjoy. Whether it be with vegetables, linoleum blocks, woodcuts, or wood engravings, the main reason for printing is no longer the illustration of books or the illuminative embellishment of manuscripts. Printing has escaped these limitations once imposed upon it and has acquired an entirely different function. It has obtained its place in the sun as a fine arts form. The printmaker is free to bring the same intense feeling and personal expression to his work as is the painter or sculptor. Printmaking today is capable of offering people a creative experience which integrates and enriches their existence.

Regardless of the tools, techniques, and materials used, the principle of relief printing remains basically the same; that is, to obtain an impression the printmaker must effect the transfer of ink from a raised surface to a sheet of paper. In creating his printing plate the artist makes one part of his plate higher than the other and determines those areas which will come into contact with the ink. When the plate is inked and placed over the paper it will then transfer the ink from the raised or relief areas to the paper, creating an impression. If we look at the prints on page 35, it will be apparent that in the print of the duck relatively little of the linoleum was cut away, while in the Saltine Warrior most of the block has been removed leaving very few raised surfaces to produce a black-line effect.

The average relief print is of an even tone with no intermediate grays or tonal qualities. Variations of middle tones, however, can be obtained simply by creating more than one printing surface. With slight variations between a number of surfaces, the unevenness of applied pressure will result in a variety of tones. Surfaces *a, c, e, g,* and *i* will produce strong color effects, while surfaces *f* and *h* will produce more graduated tones of the same color. Surfaces *b, d,* and *j* are low enough to escape being inked and will not affect the color of the paper being used.

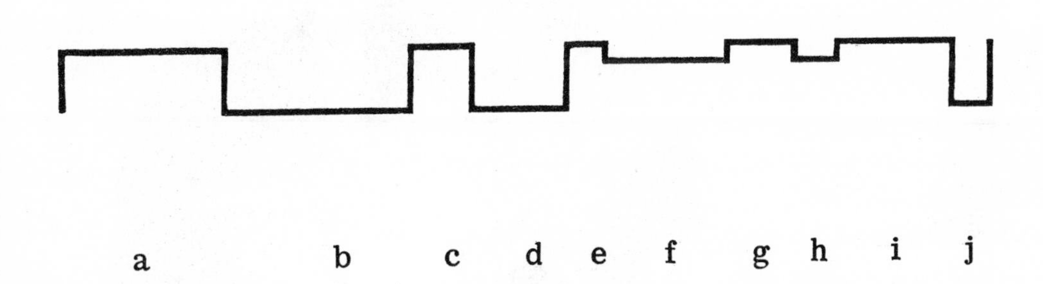

RELIEF PRINTING CAN BE AS SIMPLE AS A HANDPRINT

Almost any conceivable material, from a single finger to a sponge, piece of string, lump of clay, leaf, bottle cap, or wooden spool, if charged with ink and pressed firmly against an absorbent surface, will reproduce a line or mass effect.

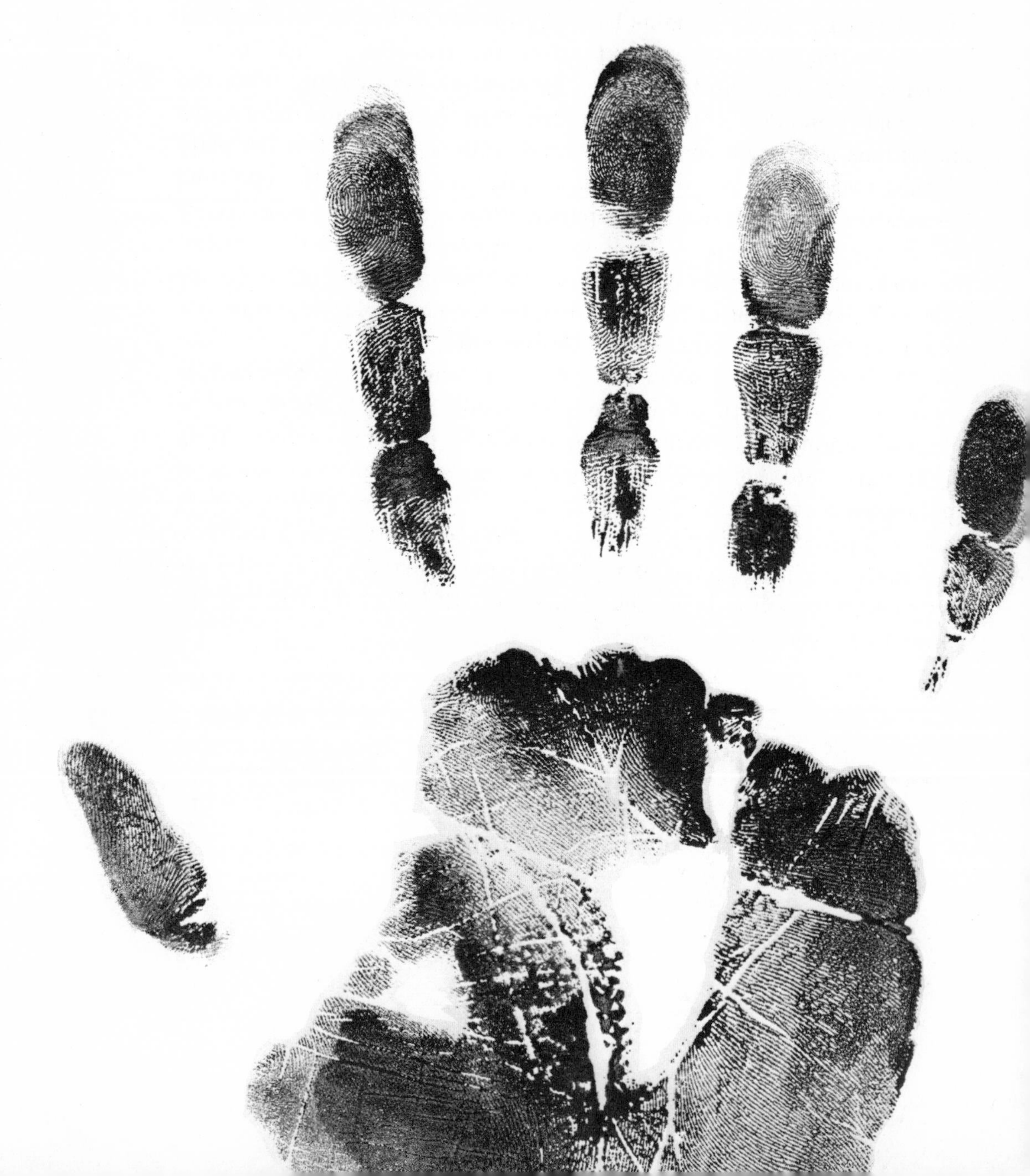

OR AS COMPLEX AS AN ALBRECHT DÜRER

requiring a high degree of technical virtuosity and the creative experiences of a great artist. Such a literal print possesses the rare quality of creditability. Or it can be abstract and highly interpretative, giving undivided attention to the creative measure of form, texture, color, and the emotions.

Courtesy of The Art Institute of Chicago, Clarence Buckingham Collection.

Printing with Natural Objects

The relief printing processes by which a print may be obtained can be divided into three broad categories. The first is printing with objects which require little or no preparation such as spools, corks, bottletops, odd pieces of wood, leaves, textured fabrics, plastic forks, and sponges. These materials usually can be found around the home or in the classroom. Consideration should be given to the selection of the objects relative to their design, affinity for ink or paint, and ability to withstand the pressure of the actual printing process. This simple printing technique can be done by children of any age level. All that one must do is apply paint to the object with a brush or sponge, or dip the object into paint, and press it onto the paper. This method of printing permits not only the free manipulation of objects in printing but also considerable experimentation with design. Almost effortlessly, children

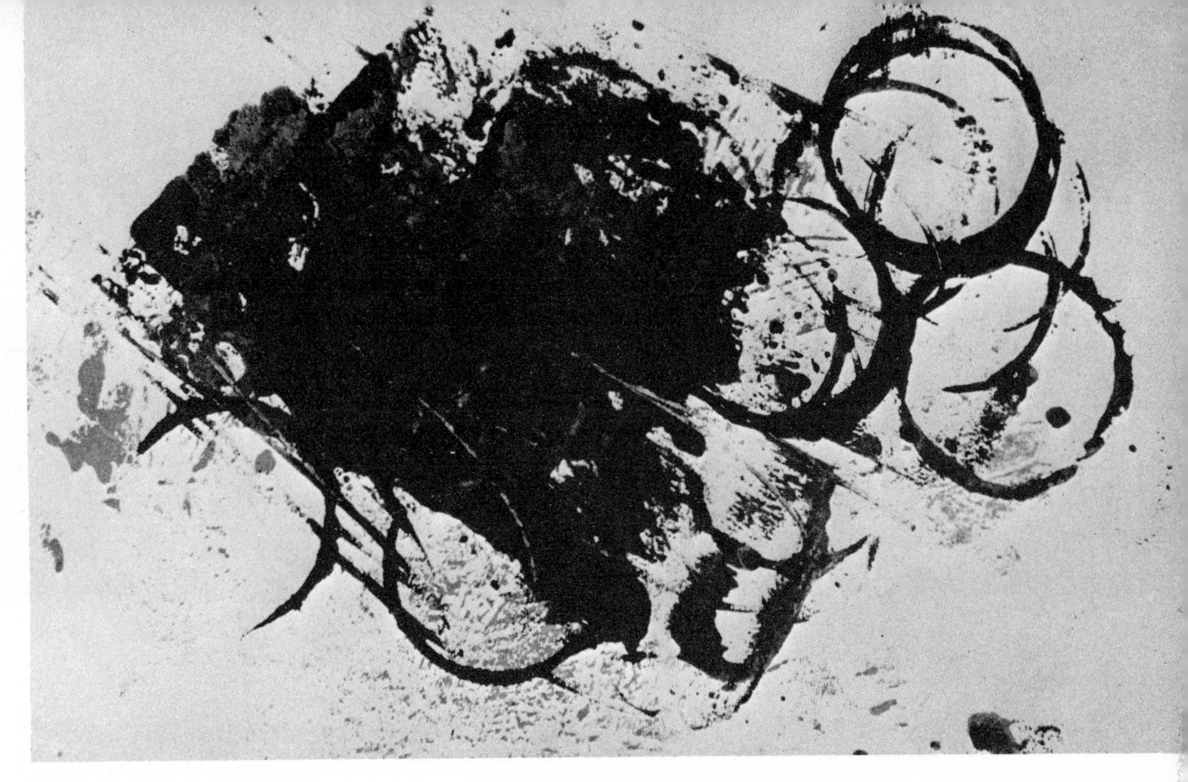

Print by a preschool child.

can experience the interrelationship of colors and motifs. With a little guidance they will be able to make repeated designs and controlled all-over patterns. Objects that are too flat to be held with the fingers, such as string, keys, or buttons, may be glued to a block of wood or the bottom of a small cardboard box. When the glue is thoroughly dry, paint can be applied to the objects with the aid of a brush or brayer.

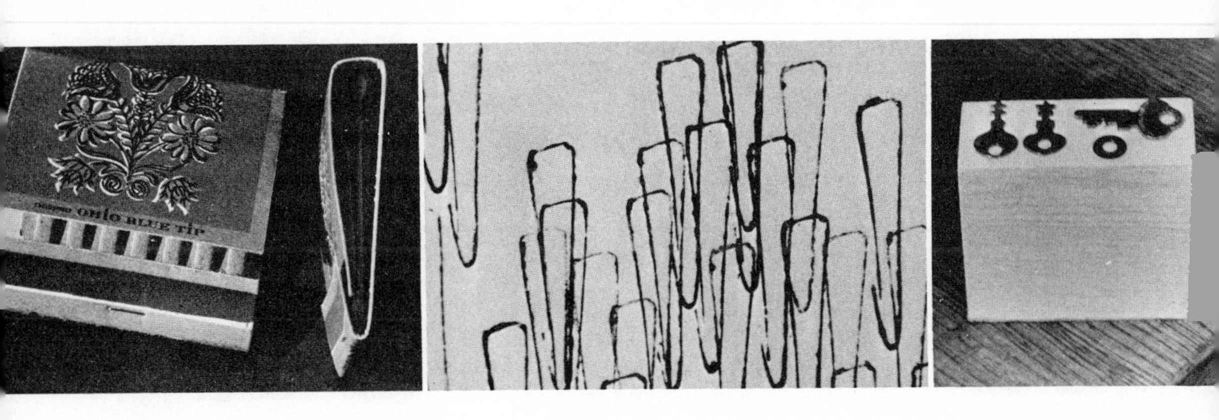

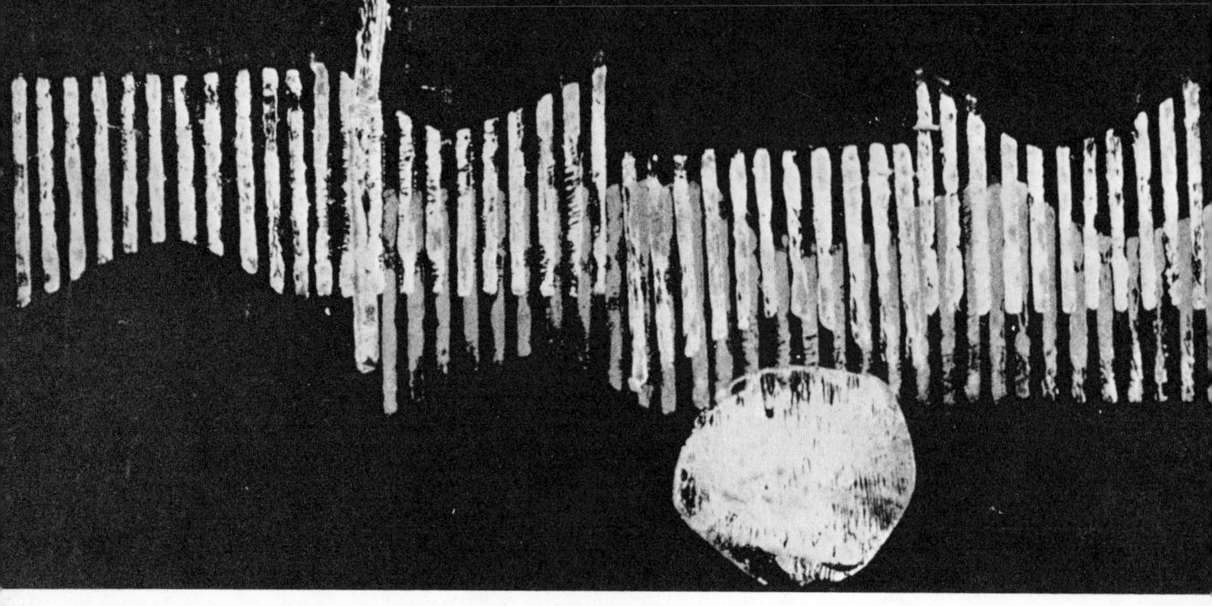

A stick print.

More advanced students may attempt to incorporate a number of different shapes and colors in their design or they may use a combination of textured objects. Those who are more adventurous may experiment with multiplication and variation of fine and heavy lines or a play of line against mass, and may even aim for tonal uniformity as well as variations by controlling the distribution of paint and the amount of pressure applied.

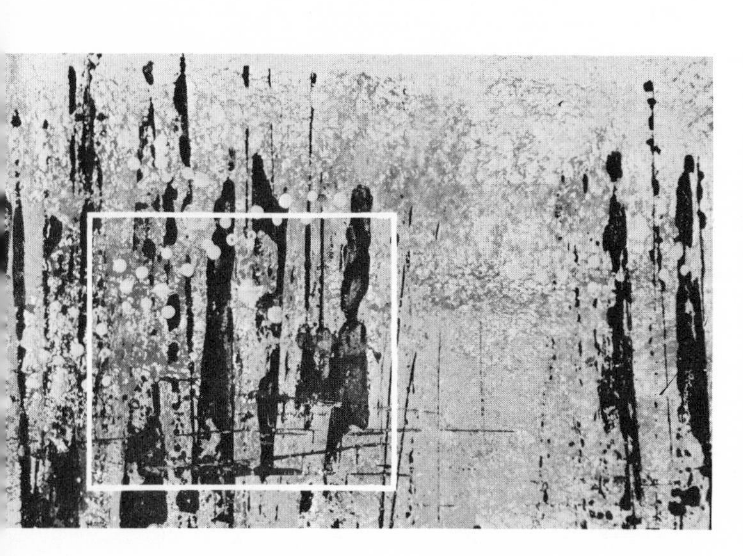

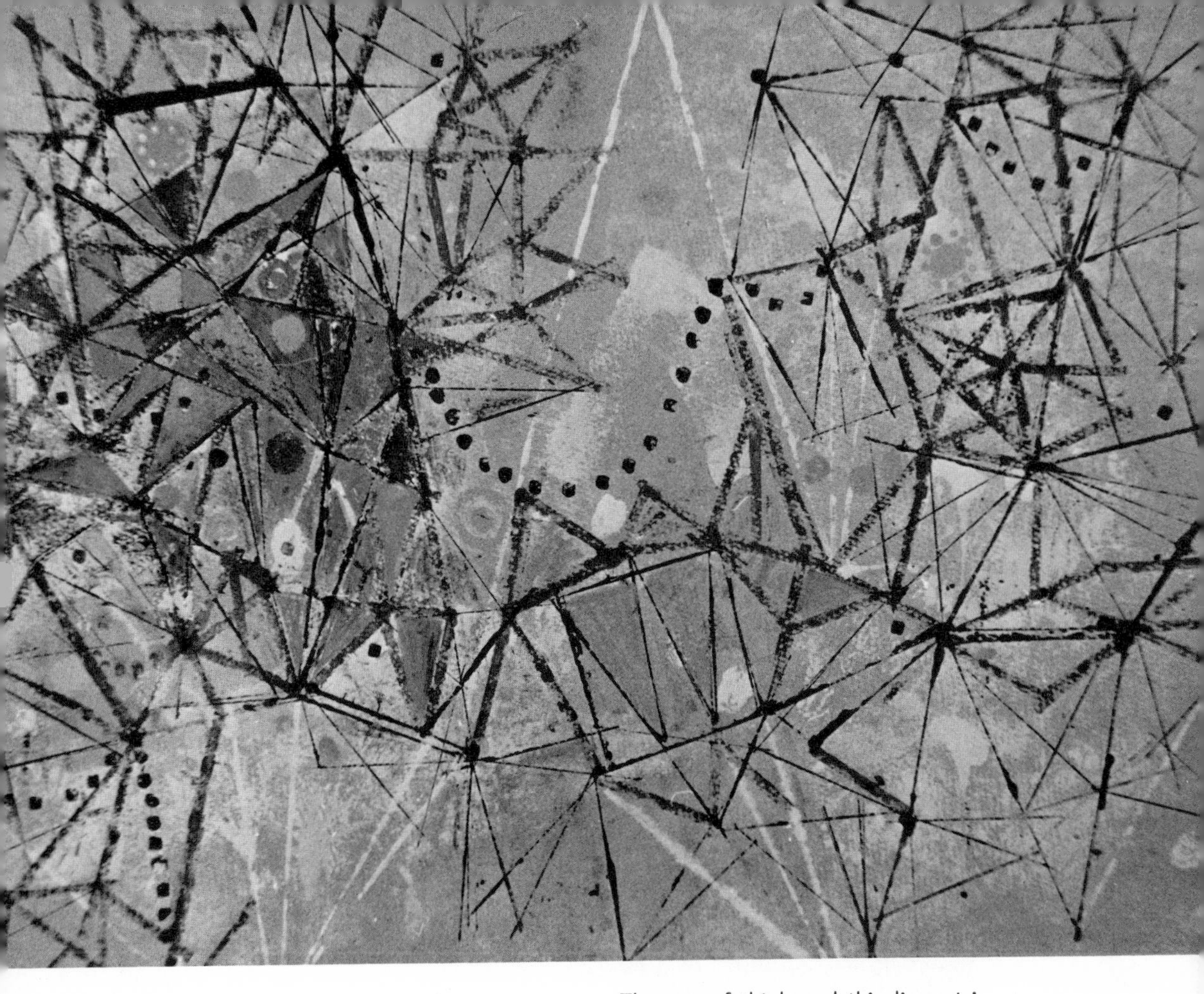

The use of thick and thin lines, triangles, and contrasting darks and lights help to symbolize the student's perception of a roller coaster. Directly applying pigment to the ground with sticks of various sizes resulted in a positive image on a subordinate background.

Recording the impression of a fish is considered fairly simple, but calls for gentle and deliberate handling. The fish is washed, brushed with a fairly thick ink, covered with a sheet of soft paper, and gently rubbed with the palm of the hand. Pulling the print is a delicate operation. The striking image of the fish is an impressive reward.

Printing-objects that are delicate, fragile, or hard to handle may be placed flat on a sheet of newspaper (used to protect the work surface) and inked by lightly rolling a brayer back and forth over the surface. Care should be taken not to ink the newspaper for it may leave a ghost impression on the finished print. A sheet of paper, usually newsprint, is then gently placed over the inked surface and pressed with the tips of the fingers or a clean brayer which is rolled evenly over the entire surface. This type of printing is spontaneous, requires a minimum amount of planning, and can be done by any age group. For a more effective print, a felt or sponge pad may be used underneath the newspaper to cushion the printing plate. If these are not available, one may use corrugated cardboard, several layers of newspaper, or discarded blotters.

Brayer printing.

Printing with a brayer can be as interesting and rewarding as the printing of odds and ends. All one need do is charge the brayer with printer's ink or paint and roll it onto the paper. Interesting effects and tonal qualities may be obtained by applying varying degrees of pressure to the brayer. The application of different colors with rollers of various sizes will also add to the design variations. For other interesting effects, the roller can be wrapped with a string which in turn is charged by rolling it over the surface of an ink slab containing paint.

Printing from Prepared Surfaces

The second major category of relief printing uses an array of materials which can be altered to create one's own original design or composition. Among the more popular materials are the traditional vegetables and fruits, as well as matboard, screen, burlap, rubber, string, wire, pipe cleaners, sandpaper, and uncoated corrugated cardboard. Using these elementary materials can be exciting and challenging. They can be cut and arranged to create pleasing designs which can be repeated any number of times and in many different combinations.

A turnip print.

The best vegetables for this purpose are those that are firm and have an interesting texture. Potatoes, carrots, turnips, celery, and radishes, as well as onions, cucumbers, cabbages, eggplants, and peppers are the most effective in printing. Apples and pears are also suitable. The fruit or vegetable should be cut in half in order to obtain a fairly flat printing surface. A paring or pocketknife or linoleum tools may be used to cut the design. Since vegetables and fruits lend themselves best to repeated design prints, perhaps the best way to charge the printing surface is to use an ink or paint pad. A dampened, folded paper towel saturated with paint also works very well. Children should be exposed to a variety of vegetables so that they may find one they can easily grasp and that has a texture suited to their interests.

Striking results may be obtained by using a variety of media. Imprinted clay and the edge of a piece of cardboard were used in creating the desired print, shown above.

Other cutout materials that have been prepared for printing, such as cardboard, rubber, sheet cork, and burlap, need only be glued down on a sturdy flat base. Consideration, of course, should be given to the design quality, or composition, in making the printing plate. These materials have many advantages and by no means should be used solely because they are available and relatively inexpensive.

This method of relief printing is advocated because it permits the student to create by utilizing the characteristics of the materials. The nature of materials has a way of suggesting design, and this should always be kept in mind. Burlap will produce an impression different from corrugated cardboard or sandpaper. A piece of cardboard, for example, will lend itself to the perforation of a paper punch, and can, therefore, give a different effect than a piece of wood. Students should be encouraged to look for different materials to use in printing. This can be fun and interesting at the same time. An endless variety of materials can be found, and the act of searching and selecting develops perception and appreciation.

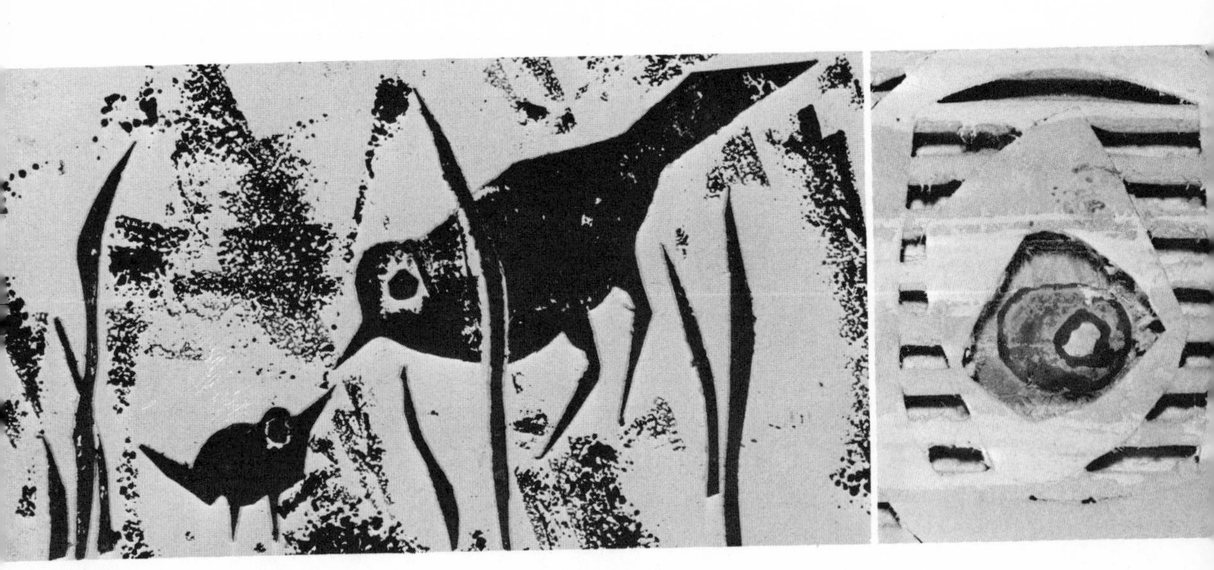

Many of the paste-down materials cannot be cut into shapes. They require a simple twisting and placing action. Such materials as string, wire, pipe cleaners, and some of the previously mentioned objects such as keys, washers, buttons, seeds, beans, and sticks of various sizes fall into this category. In making paste-down plates it is very important to keep the level of the printing surface as uniform as possible. Otherwise only the relatively high surfaces will print. If metal objects will not take the paint, they may be sprayed with a lacquer or rubbed vigorously with steel wool or a piece of emery cloth. This gives the metal a rough surface which will receive the paint.

The technique of printing this type of plate is similar to that used with the natural objects. The large plates are best charged with a brayer, and, although no press is absolutely necessary, an available press will give the artist a great deal more control and a better chance of pulling a fine print. If a press is to be used, obviously one must be careful of the type of objects incorporated in the making of the plate. Wire and metal objects can mar the rubber rollers.

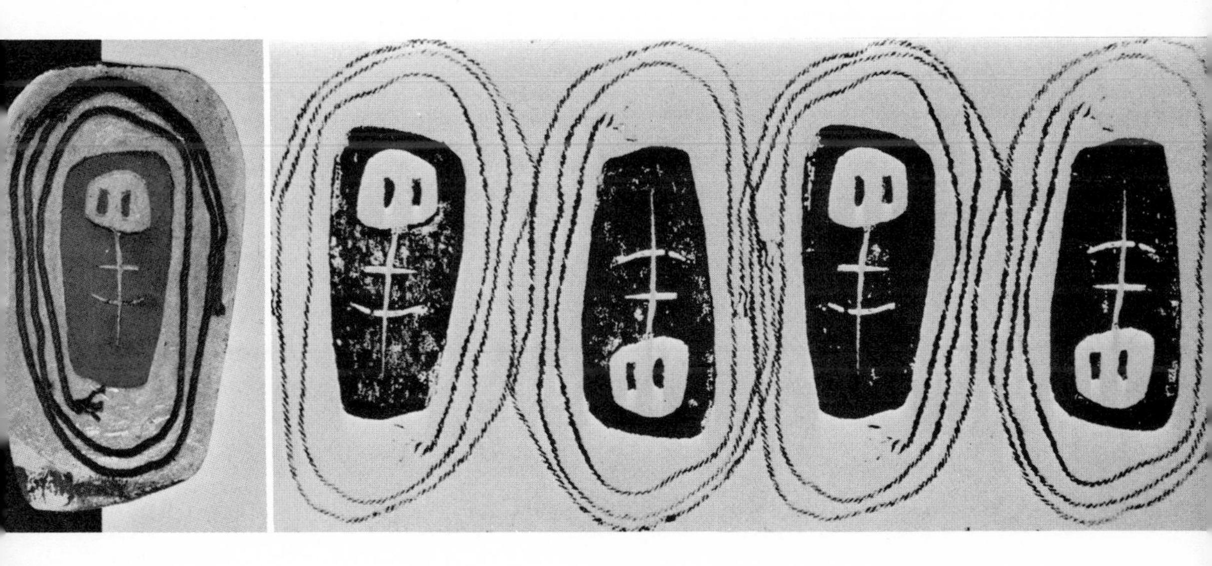

An interesting collagraphic plate and the resultant print.

Clay and plastiline make good printing surfaces. Even the youngest children will find these materials interesting and fascinating. A lump of clay may be pressed against the table in order to produce a flat surface, which is then impressed with the aid of a pencil, sticks, buttons, or the like. The clay is then given a coating of paint and pressed to the paper in much the same manner as are vegetables.

An alternate method would be to roll out the clay or plastiline with a rolling pin, making a flat pancake about an inch thick. An image is then inscribed or impressed into the slab of clay. After the clay slab has been charged with paint, a piece of print paper is placed over the slab's inked surface and gently pressed with the tips of the fingers, moving from the center of the clay slab to the outer edges. The print is then carefully pulled and set aside to dry.

Printer's ink, paint, or dye can be applied to the printing objects in a number of different ways. The most conventional is to place paint on a palette, glass slab, or sheet of masonite across which a brayer is rolled until properly charged. Then the brayer is rolled across the surface of the printing plate. Ink, dye, or paint may also be applied by brush, sponge, rag, or with the aid of an ink pad.

The linear quality of string creates abstract and figurative prints. After being glued to a piece of masonite or cardboard surface in desired design patterns, the string is inked, and then printed. Heavy cord, wire, and pipe cleaners may also be used. Each has a quality all its own and adds an interesting variety of lines to the print. In string printing, much of the plate's background cannot help being inked; thus the ink is unintentionally transmitted to the areas of the finished print which are not to be printed.

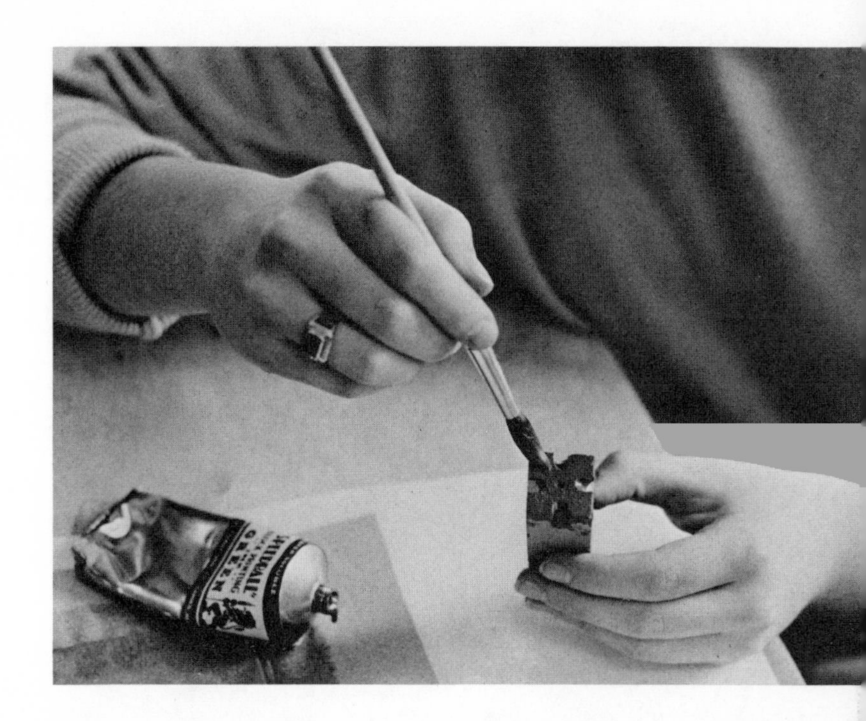

Pigment may be applied with a brush or a saturated pad.

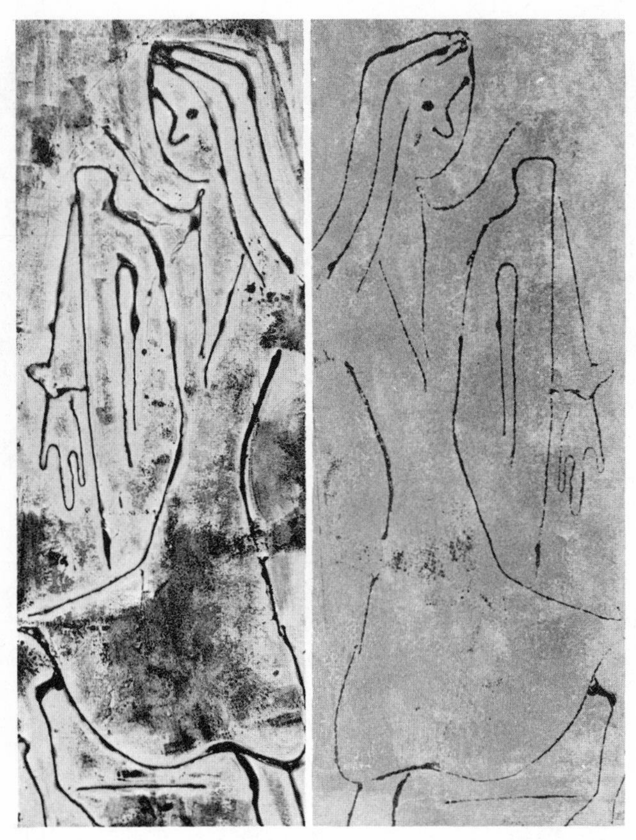

A string print.

Bold linear prints can also be created by squeezing thick rubber cement, or dripping lacquer or any similar adhesive, onto a sheet of cardboard, masonite, wood, or glass. After the cement or lacquer is thoroughly dry, it is inked and printed as you would print any relief plate. The preparation of the printing plate may be accomplished by either of two methods. The first is to create the impression spontaneously as you squeeze the rubber cement onto the actual printing surface. The other method involves placing a predesigned brush drawing or pencil sketch beneath a glass plate and tracing it through the glass onto the printing surface. If the rubber cement or lacquer impression is not sufficiently thick when dry, it will permit large areas of the unwanted background to print, all but obscuring the line quality being printed.

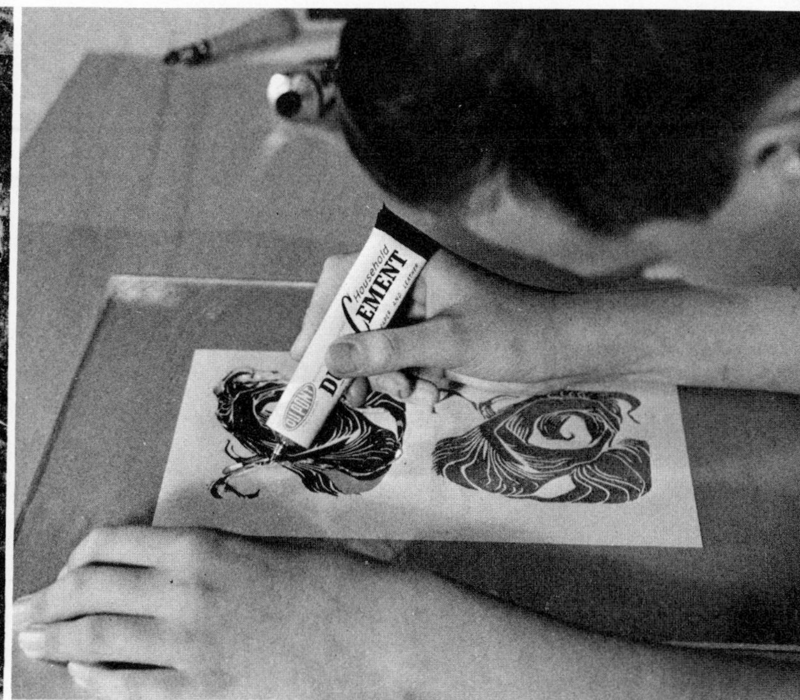

Printing with rubber cement.

Printing from Carved Surfaces

The third approach to relief printing is the traditional method of cutting into the flat surface of a block of linoleum, wood, or similar material. The cutting and gouging creates shapes, textures, and patterns. The areas which are not a part of the design are removed, leaving the area to be printed standing in relief. Of the three methods of relief printing, printing from carved surfaces requires the greatest amount of time, patience, and knowledge of tools and techniques. For this reason, the cutting process is usually reserved for the preadolescents and older students.

One of the best ways of introducing this third method to the students is to have them, initially, work with linoleum, thereby gaining cutting experience and learning to integrate creative ideas and craftsmanship. Linoleum printing is probably the most widely used of the cutting processes. The characteristics of the medium make it easy to cut, and one obtains a strong black-and-white contrast. Linoleum's lack of grain permits cutting in any direction, with almost any sharp instrument. Linoleum may be cut with various gouges, linoleum cutters, or wood carving tools. Many students prefer using the veiner to score the preliminary outline; the larger areas are then more conveniently removed with the gouges. The pliability of linoleum makes it easy to secure a clear print. Should the linoleum appear stiff and too hard to cut, it may be heated for a few minutes. This causes it to soften and facilitates the cutting.

It is always best that the students use a fairly large piece of linoleum and think of large, simple areas for their designs. This will tend to eliminate intricate lines and details that are so difficult to control.

Paraffin, soap, and casein prints

There are a number of other easy-to-cut media for beginners, some of which may be used even in the lower grades. Paraffin and soap are impressionable materials which can be marked with a pencil, pin, tongue depressor, spoon, or fork. Since paraffin and soap have a tendency to be water-resistant, it is best to use printer's ink or an oil-base paint in place of the usual water-base paints. Casein printing plates can also be made. The cutting surface is prepared by coating a piece of plywood or masonite with several thick layers of casein paint. Cutting is made easier by keeping the prepared surface damp. Many interesting effects may be obtained by pressing such textured materials as burlap and screen into the paint when it is still in its plastic state, allowing it to dry, and then printing.

Plaster block prints

A slab of plaster may also be used as a printing plate. The design or image is cut into the smooth surface of the plaster with a knife, wood gouges, or linoleum cutters. It is usually advisable to size the finished plaster block with a coat of shellac before printing, to prevent it from absorbing too much of the paint. Plaster slabs can be made by pouring a mixture of equal amounts of water and plaster of Paris into a cardboard box and allowing it to "set" and dry. Other inexpensive materials that may be used are plywood, matboard, chip board, and corrugated cardboard.

The materials mentioned above, as well as wood and lucite, are inked and printed in much the same manner as most relief prints. The paper, however, may be placed over the inked plate and rubbed gently with a burnisher, baren, or the bowl of a large spoon. The smaller blocks may be pressed against the face of the paper, the pressure being applied by the student's standing gently on the block. A third method may be the use of a screw-type press or washer wringer. A press, as we have previously mentioned, is not absolutely necessary but is highly recommended for the beginner because of his inability to use the hand, foot, or spoon method. Prints produced without a press are often too light or uneven in tone, and can be very disheartening.

Almost any kind of paper may be used for the print. The less expensive newsprint, tissue paper, drawing and construction paper are quite satisfactory. The soft Japanese rice paper, however, still proves to be the best. Cloth may also be used. When printing on cloth, it is advisable to cover the table surface with felt padding or several layers of papers to cushion the printing surface so that the paint readily penetrates the fabric.

Any water-soluble ink or paint that is easy to clean up is highly recommended, but the enamels, lacquers, textiles, and the newer plastic paints are also satisfactory. Textile paint, which is a fast color, is especially recommended for printing on fabrics. It must be remembered, however, that the appropriate solvents are to be used in cleaning up.

In creating ideas for a print it is best that the creations not be completed in detail on paper and meticulously traced onto the block to be cut. It is more advisable, and quite permissible, to improvise thumbnail sketches or rough drafts, providing these are not copied exactly in the completed print. A good printmaker allows a margin for suggestions likely to be derived from the characteristics of the block, and which may be incorporated in the design.

"Snared" by Robert Marx, Syracuse University, is a colored linoleum print. Most of the block was removed leaving a few dynamic lines and forms to depict the struggle of a fish that has been caught. *Collection, The Museum of Modern Art, New York.*

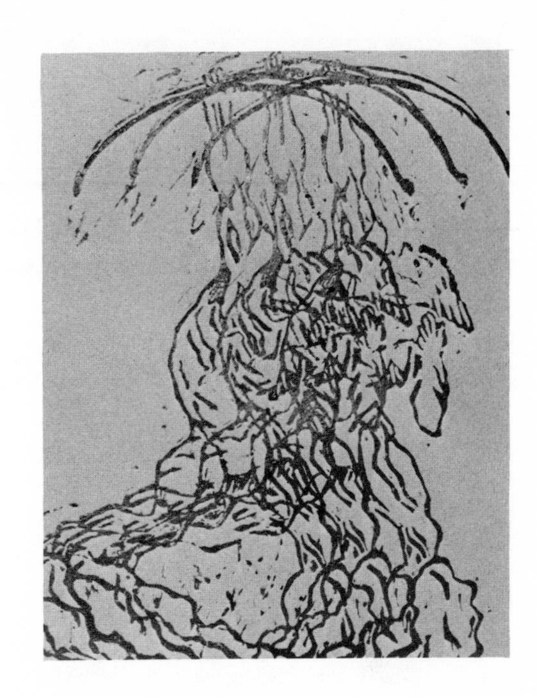

Black line, triple image prints above, white line print below.

The prints above were made with the copper foil plate shown at top right. The one in the center is a monoprint created by inking the sheet of copper, placing it with the ink down on a sheet of paper, and scribing the image with a pencil. The print at the left was reproduced by inking the imprinted plate and printing. The interesting effect of the Trojan head at the right was achieved by printing the same linoleum block twice with two different colors, slightly off register.

Woodcuts

Woodcuts are perhaps the oldest of the formal carved relief printing methods. They were prepared by skilled craftsmen to be used by manuscript printers long before Johann Gutenberg invented the separate movable-block printing press. There is some evidence of the use of woodcuts in the fine Coptic textiles of the seventh century. These first woodcuts were usually imitations of line drawings reproduced to the color specifications of the publisher.

Wood engraving, a more highly refined process, followed shortly, and reached the height of its popularity in the late nineteenth century. Engravings are made by cutting into the end-grain of a block of fairly hard wood which has been cut horizontally from a tree trunk. Woodcuts, on the other hand, are made by cutting into a block whose grain runs parallel to the length of the board; thus they are much easier to cut. Since wood engraving is highly complicated and requires special, costly tools, it is an unsatisfactory process for the novice. Simple wood reliefs, on the other hand, can be done by very young children.

Woodcut printing experiences are made available to even the youngest child through the use of dowels, square pieces of fir, and pine sticks of various sizes. These should be long enough to facilitate handling during the actual printing. Designs may be made by cutting into the end-grain of the wood with a sloyd knife, a saw, round and/or triangular files, as well as by drilling and pounding holes into it. It is best to allow the wood blocks to soak for a while in water before printing; otherwise they will be too absorbent, soaking in the paint and producing faint prints. The blocks are inked in much the same way as are the natural objects described in the first method of relief printing.

The art of the woodcut lies within reach of elementary school children. The technique is very simple and need not require a high degree of skill, knowledge, or expensive equipment. The print below was made by a nine-year-old from soft pine wood without any preliminary drawing at all. The wood surface was first blackened to facilitate seeing the cuts as they were made. This simple, direct technique resulted in a free, dynamic, and spontaneous looking print.

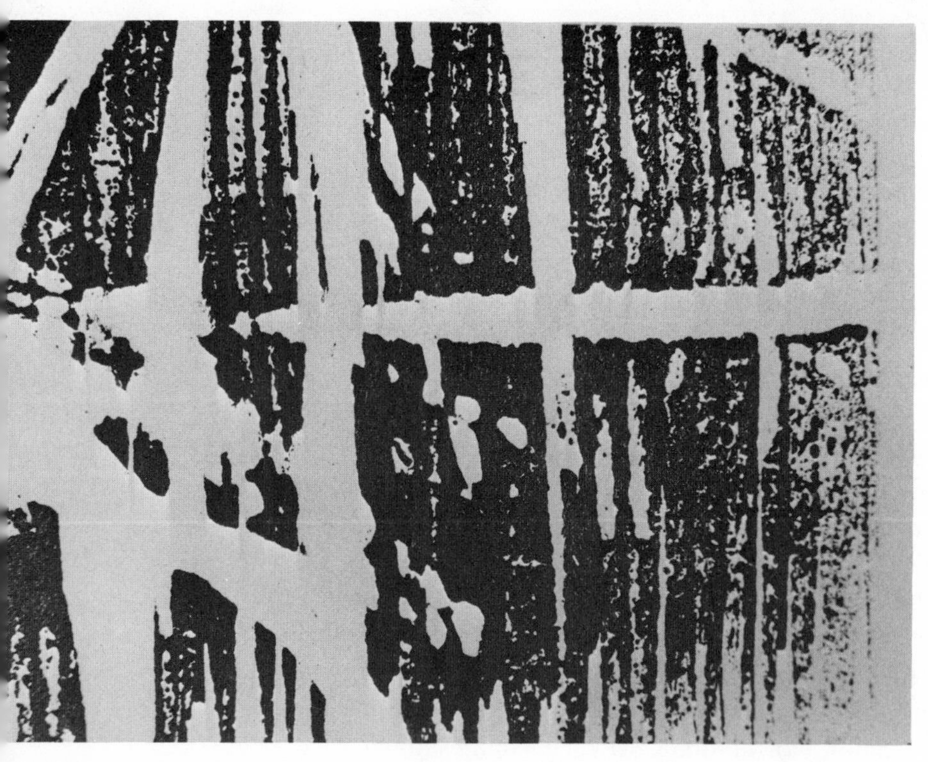

A woodcut by a high school student.

The traditional woodcutting method is unquestionably the most suitable for junior and senior high students. It requires care and patience, and challenges the students to think and to combine their creative powers with physical dexterity; yet it does not require any skill or technical knowledge beyond their reach.

The grain of wood has a predominant influence on the character of the resulting print. Although cutting with the grain is much easier, cutting against the grain produces vigorous and interesting effects and is certainly advocated. Fairly soft woods such as beech, bass, sycamore, cherry, apple, and pear permit the use of fine line and various textures, which may be made by pounding screen and nails into the flat printing surface. Students should be encouraged to experiment with knives, chisels, and gouges; by acquainting themselves with the effects of the cutting tools, they will understand better how the materials respond.

"Blue Veil" by Alfred Sessler, University of Wisconsin, represents a refined woodcut done in many colors. It is typical of the process used by the Japanese of making a multicolor print from a single plate.

Students should be encouraged to experiment by exploring the numerous methods of printing. They should be given the opportunity to produce black line, white line, and double-image prints; to use several blocks of various sizes, shapes, and textures; to achieve multicolor effects by using the same block with different colors, printing on different colored papers, or pasting down areas of colored paper and printing with the original block; and to deliberately off-register.

The paper to be printed upon may be given various other preliminary background treatments. It may be painted with a brush, sprayed, or rolled with a brayer which has been charged with an appropriate background color.

Linoleum blocks or woodcuts characteristically lend themselves to the Japanese process of making a multicolor print from a single plate. Various colors are applied with a brush on the different areas of the plate and printed exactly like a single-color run. High school students can attempt colored prints by using a separate block for each color. They should begin with a two-colored block print, reserving the more complicated process until after they have mastered the technique of multicolor printing. An interesting procedure for insuring good registration is to press the image of the finished first block onto the second, leaving a clear impression to act as a guide by which to cut.

It is a very good idea to take a proof of the block at different intervals of the actual carving, in order to observe one's progress. This may best be done either by making a print of the unfinished plate or by placing a thin sheet of paper over the top of the impression and making a rubbing by going over the entire surface with a soft lead pencil or chalk. A disadvantage of the latter method is the failure to get the reverse image, which would be a truer proof of the final print.

2

The Stencil Printing Process

Stencil printing is considered by many to be a relative newcomer to the field of graphic arts. But as an artistic technique its history goes back to the cave wall paintings of prehistoric Europe. Cro-Magnon man, some 20,000 years ago, incorporated in his brush paintings a technique of blowing pulverized pigments, usually iron and manganese oxides, through a reed or a hollow bone to outline the contours of his animal drawings. The means of projection was much like our modern airbrush technique. This same "air painting" technique was also used

to blow colored pigment over the hand, which corresponds to our mask stencil. Such hand impressions are frequently found among the paleolithic reindeer and horse paintings in the Font de Guame cave at Les Eyzies, France, and also at Lascaux.

There are a number of methods which follow the principle of stencil printing. The air painting, spray, or spatter technique of the prehistoric man is but one variation of the process. Another example is the use of an open mesh or perforated surface through which paint is forced. The ancient Chinese artists wove such a mesh out of human hair and used its screen-like surface to decorate their pottery and fabrics.* More recently, a method of producing a stencil on film has been perfected. The basic principle, however, remains the same. The methods described here are easily adapted to school use.

The Stencil-Screen Processes

There are two distinct techniques in the stencil-screen printing process. The one in which paint is forced through the clear opening of a stencil or around its outer margins we shall refer to as stenciling. That in which the paint is forced through a screen or mesh surface we shall refer to as silk screen printing or serigraphy.

* James A. Schinneller, *Art: Search and Self-Discovery* (Scranton, Pennsylvania: International Textbook Company, 1961).

Like relief printing, stenciling can be introduced as a simple process starting with natural objects which require little or no preparation. Then we can move gradually toward a method which requires a minimum amount of planning, then to a variation of more complex methods requiring a greater amount of time, considerable control of the medium, and a high degree of technical knowledge and skill.

Simple Stencil Printing

It is important to begin with a simple process. Children may be encouraged to choose an object which will make an interesting motif. Leaves, coins, keys, or any other objects with interesting shapes will do, as long as they are flat forms devoid of intricate detail. The object may then be placed in the center of a sheet of paper and with the aid of an old toothbrush, a spatula, and tempera paint the motif may be transformed into a simple screen print.

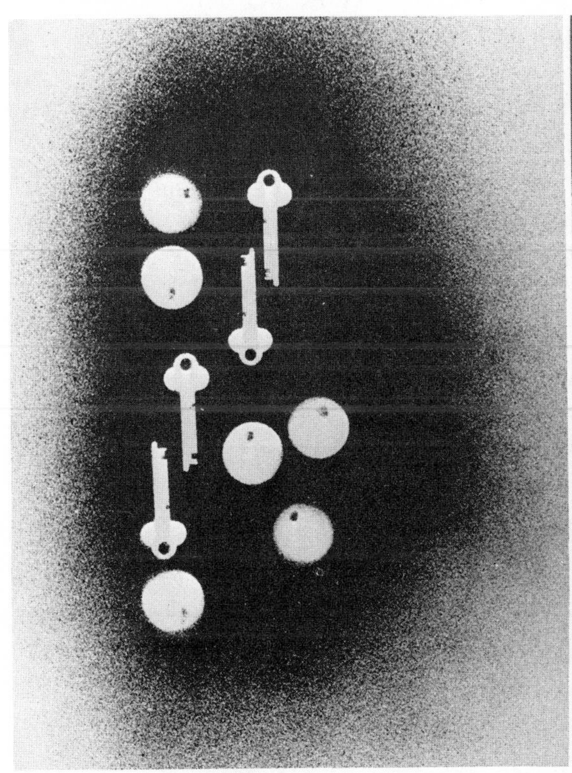

In this process, the paint is applied to the toothbrush by dipping the tips of the brush bristles into it, being careful not to load the brush too heavily. Any surplus paint may be removed by lightly scraping the bristles along the inside rim of the paint container. The toothbrush is then held about six inches over the stencil-object, perpendicular to the paper. The bristles are gently stroked by drawing the spatula toward oneself. The bristles spring back, spattering paint over the motif and onto the paper. This process is continued until the desired effect is obtained. A wire screen may be used in place of the spatula. In this case the toothbrush is rubbed briskly against the screen, which is held parallel to and approximately six inches above the paper. For the very young, the wire screen method may be the easiest and, therefore, the best to use.

For most children, stenciling will undoubtedly be new, inspiring, and fascinating. They should be allowed to experiment by holding the toothbrush or wire screen at varying distances from the paper, by using different colored paints, by repeating the motifs, and by applying various quantities of paint. When changing colors, one must first be certain to clean the brush to prevent unintentional mixing of colors.

It is best to choose a single motif at first, repeating it over and over in a straight line and later in rows of lines creating an allover pattern. Later children may be encouraged to print their motif in a combination of different positions: turning the stencil-object upside down and sideways, repeating the motif in irregular as well as regular intervals, and trying a variation of repeated patterns.

Combination brush-stencil technique and stick-printing overlay in black by a college student.

Children may next attempt to create their own motifs by cutting designs from sheets of cardboard with a pair of scissors. These designs are placed on paper in any of the interesting arrangements previously experienced and then spattered over. Papers of different color and texture may be used for the background. Children should, however, have the opportunity to select their own papers and paints. This method is a satisfactory approach to creative expression whereby they are given the opportunity to explore the basic laws of design. They are encouraged to experiment with value, color intervals, contrasts, balance, and alternating shapes, sizes, and colors.

Another example of the simple stencil technique is open or cutout stencil printing. In this method, voids are cut into special types of material through which the paint is applied.

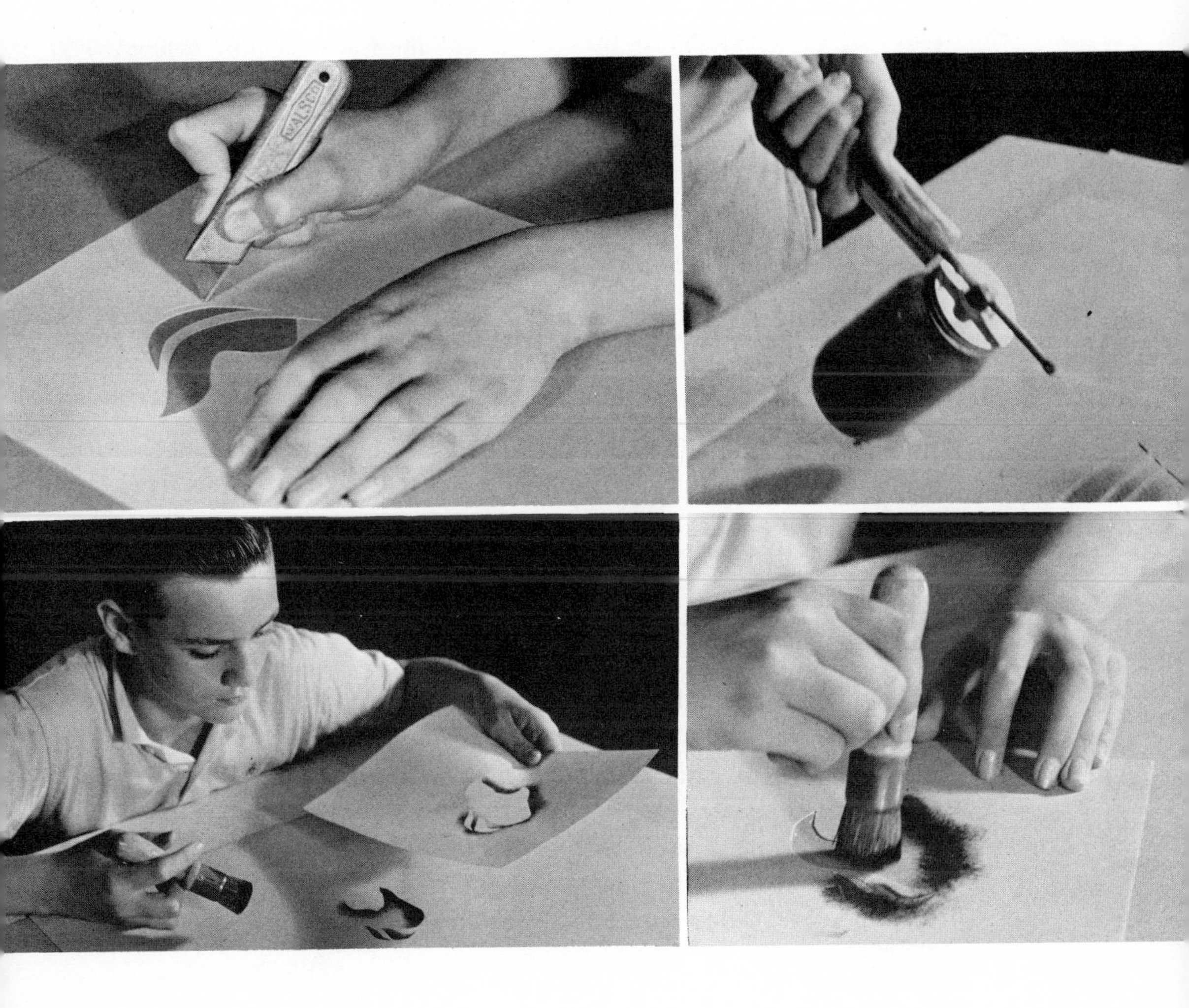

Cutout stencil printing can be as simple as cutting a design directly into a piece of waterproof or semiwaterproof paper. No predesigned sketch is necessary. The stencil is placed over the area to be printed and paint is then rubbed through the opening with a sponge or brush. It is important that the paint have the proper consistency. If it is not thick enough it will run and bleed, and if it is too thick it will leave an excessive residue of paint on the stencil and on the area being printed. The actual stenciling should be done with care in order not to move the stencil unintentionally, smudging the print or damaging the stencil plate.

For the first project, experiment with a single motif, creating a simple compact design without detail or minute parts. If the transform of objects in nature to design is desired, it is wise to attempt to adopt the symbolic rather than what seems to be the realistic forms of the objects. It is important to study the objects thoroughly, to learn to understand and to be able to interpret their most unusual and essential characteristics so that they may be recreated and symbolized, not copied.

After a design has been created, it is transferred to a stencil material such as a sheet of aluminum or copper foil, waxed stencil paper, or a piece of cardboard that has been coated with varnish, shellac, or spray wax. With a pair of scissors the designed area is cut out. The use of EZ or Sanford's stencil paper, which is wax coated, transparent, and waterproof, eliminates the transfer-drawing step and permits cutting directly into the stencil with a brisket or stencil knife. In cutting a stencil, allow at least a two-inch margin around the design to protect the print surface.

The finished stencil is placed over the paper to be printed and held firmly in place. The color is then applied with a brush by pulling it

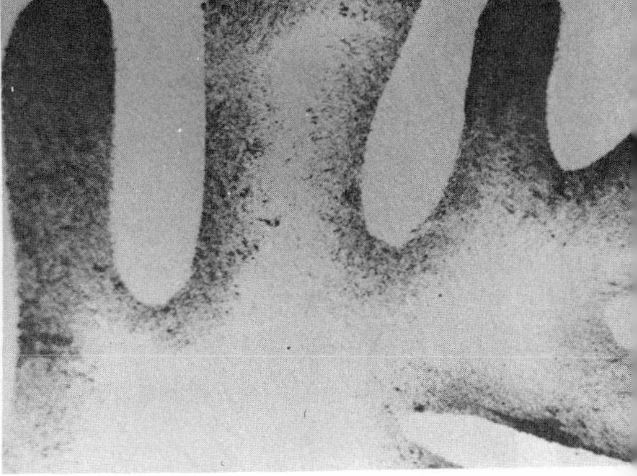

across the stencil opening from the outer edges toward the center. Although a number of applicators may be used, special stencil brushes are recommended. These are inexpensive, short, stiff-bristle brushes designed especially for the stencil technique.

Different paints or inks may be used. If the printing is to be done on paper, stencil inks and water-base paints are suitable. One may also choose to use wax crayons, Cray-Pas, chalk, or another coloring matter. If the printing is to be done on fabric, it is best to use textile dyes or tube oil paints.

This simple motif process, itself, has little interest, but it teaches children the principle of cutout stencil printing and allows them to recreate their own world of art. These simple motifs may later be combined in different ways to create border and allover design patterns. Using this basic approach one can experiment with the infinite variations of the technique. By changing or substituting the paints and surfaces to be printed upon and adding to the number of stencils, all manner of results and surprises can occur.

There are two basic techniques of applying paint with a stencil brush. The first and possibly the easiest method is one in which the printing area within the stencil opening is not filled completely with paint. The brush is stroked or daubed across a mere fraction of the open area starting from the outline of the motif and working toward the center. This technique is more effective in larger open designs.

The second technique is to apply the paint evenly over the entire open area. Several light applications of paint prove to be much better than attempting one heavy application. An interesting variation of this technique would be to attempt a chiaroscuro effect by starting from the outside of the open area with a heavy application of color and gradually applying a smaller amount of paint as you work toward the center of the area. More experienced students utilize the chiaroscuro technique with remarkable virtuosity in effecting tonalities.

If a print with more than one motif is desired, a separate stencil is required for each motif, which is best cut from a separate piece of stencil paper. If a single motif calls for more than one color, a separate stencil is also cut for each color. Although in some cases the same stencil can be used for different colors, it is more convenient to cut separate ones, inasmuch as these stencils are inexpensive and take very little time to cut. The separate stencils are later combined to create the final composite print.

When a number of stencils are to be used in a single print, the main consideration becomes proper registration, which must be thought out carefully before the stencils are cut. To assure proper registration, secure the design to a cutting board, piece of masonite, or plate glass. Draw a right angle on the registration board two to three inches above and to the left of the design. This right angle should be made dark enough to be seen easily through the transparent stencil paper, because it will serve as a registration guide in cutting the number of needed stencils. The first piece of stencil paper is placed to fit into the right angle and secured with masking tape. The first stencil plate is then made in one of two ways. It is either traced and cut, or cut directly from the stencil paper, with a stencil or mat knife. This is done for each successive color, from the lightest to the darkest. Each stencil is carefully numbered consecutively to facilitate proper registration during the printing process. If the stencils are to be cut directly from the original sketch, it would prevent the mutilation of the design if the design and registration guide were placed underneath a piece of plate glass or plexiglas.

Registration of the printing is carried out in much the same way. The surface to be printed on, that is, paper or fabric, is secured to a

drawing board. The first stencil is then placed in the desired position and with two pieces of masking tape the right angle is recreated on the printing surface. Using masking tape to create the right angles, instead of drawing them, will eliminate any guide lines on the finished print; on fabrics, such lines are difficult to remove. The first stencil is made secure and is printed. The procedure is then continued until each stencil has been consecutively printed. If the printing surface is a fabric which has been printed with textile paints, it is left to dry for at least twenty-four hours, and set with a hot iron at 350 degrees. A damp pressing cloth which has been dipped in white vinegar may be applied in the pressing to aid in setting and fixing the colors.

It is well to keep in mind that often there must be ties to hold the stencil together. This is especially true if there are to be floating center pieces. It is therefore recommended that the designs be as simple as possible. Quality does not necessarily result from complexity, but it does result from concentration, consideration, and concern. Stenciling with care will result in a perfect print and greater satisfaction.

Stenciling is a medium of expression peculiar and appropriate to the characteristics of the materials and techniques involved. It is chosen by those who have a love for its possibilities, not a lack of, or talent for, other techniques.

Silk Screen and Serigraphy

The process in which the design is printed through a stencil that has an opening supported by a mesh-screen (usually silk, organdy,

Fish (silk screen drapery design) by Harvey Schaefer.

"Trojan Horse" (serigraph) by Dean Meeker, University of Wisconsin.

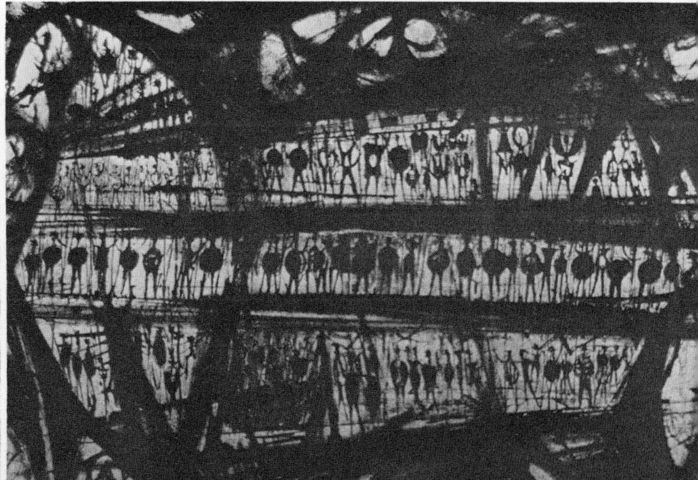

crinoline, or marquisette stretched tightly across the opening) is basically a silk screen process. There are many variations on this basic method, each determined by its purposes and dependent upon the types of stencils and pigments used in the printing.

The process of silk screening has been in use in America as a medium for applied designs and posters for approximately fifty years. It was introduced as a fine arts medium for printmakers, however, less than thirty years ago. Anthony Velonis, as head of the New York City Graphic Division of the WPA Federal Arts Project during President Franklin D. Roosevelt's administration, first gave impetus to the development of fine arts silk screen printing into the form that we know today. Among others who have contributed to its development are Carl Zigrosser, Hyman Warsager, Guy MacCoy, and Harry Sternberg. Carl Zigrosser, as Curator of Prints at the Philadelphia Museum of Art, was the first to make the distinction between silk screen as a commercial medium and as a fine arts medium. He originated the term "serigraphy," which is applied to the silk screen process when referring to the field of fine arts. We shall not press this distinction when discussing the various techniques which may be employed in the public schools; throughout this section on stencil printing the term "silk screen" will include both uses. To be cognizant of the two different uses is sufficient.

The use of silk screen printing as an educational means in public school art programs is comparatively new. Yet, it is already extremely popular with children of all age levels. It offers stimulating opportunities ranging from the development of dexterity and technical skills to understanding and appreciation, and it is an outlet for creative expression.

Ordinarily the cutout stencil technique produces a distinct, clean-cut edge between areas of color but does not lend itself to detailed design of unusual textures or blotch effects. It is suited to conceptions in large, flat areas rather than in dotted or dry brush texture areas. The silk screen method offers prints composed only of simple and bold masses, yet lends itself to a great degree of freedom in craftsmanship. The color range, relationships, and sensitivity depend, of course, on the number and types of stencils employed. In the experimental crucifixion, on page 61, seven separate stencils were used. The transparency of various colors accounts for additional color values.

Simple Silk Screen Printing

Silk screen printing has always been a relatively complex process requiring a great amount of complicated equipment and demanding a reasonably comprehensive degree of technical knowledge and skill. Recently, however, the silk screen printing technique has undergone considerable modification, which makes it suitable for most school children.

To introduce the principle of silk screening, all one needs is an embroidery hoop, coarse marquisette, fingerpaint, a pencil or crayon, a sheet of fairly stiff oaktag, a piece of surface print paper (newsprint, manila or construction paper), a four-inch piece of cardboard, and a pair of scissors. A simple design much smaller than the diameter of the embroidery hoop is drawn on the stiff oaktag and cut out with a pair of scissors. The design is then placed beneath the hoop over which the marquisette has been stretched. Next, a generous deposit of paint is placed at one end of the hoop and pulled across the stencil opening with a piece of cardboard held at a forty-five degree angle. If the paint is not evenly distributed over the entire opening it may be pulled back across the stencil. Then, while the surface paper is firmly held to the table, the embroidery hoop and stencil are gently pulled away from the surface paper, revealing the print.

There are many variations of this extraordinarily simple process. The printing frame, which was represented by the embroidery hoop in the technique described previously, can be made by the more advanced children out of mat board or heavy cardboard. With either a pair of scissors or a utility knife, cut a mat with at least a three-inch border. Tape one end of a piece of marquisette or crinoline securely to the back of the mat with the threads running parallel to the frame. Then stretch the screen to remove the slack, and tape the opposite end. Finish the two remaining sides in the same way. The screen should overlap the mat opening by at least an inch on each side. A simple wooden frame can be made out of four pieces of two-inch by one-fourth, one-half, or one-inch wood. The joints may be mitred, or they may be

jointed at right angles with the aid of glue and nails, screws, or screw angles placed at each of the four corners. The screen may be either tacked or stapled to the wooden frame. Begin by tacking or stapling in the center of one of the sides, alternately tacking either side of the center until the procedure is completed. The tacks or staples should be approximately two inches apart.

Ready-made frames in many sizes may be purchased from art supply stores. Painter's-canvas stretcher bars may also be used. The completed frame is best when hinged to a baseboard a little wider and longer than the frame itself. This will facilitate the registration when printing more than one color. The use of loose pin hinges will allow for easy removal from the baseboard for cleaning purposes.

A serigraph by a six-year-old made with a cardboard frame, marquisette, crayon block-out, finger paint, and a cardboard squeegee, combined with a great deal of imagination and self-determination.

To prevent the seepage of paint through the crevice between the screen and the frame, the inside face of the frame and the adjacent portion of screen is taped with gummed or masking paper. The gummed paper is cut to size, folded in two lengthwise, and taped, one half to the inside of the frame and the other half to the screen. A coat of varnish or shellac may be applied to secure an airtight frame.

The design to be printed may be cut directly from thin sheet-metals, parchment, EZ or Sanford's stencil paper; or it may be drawn on a sheet of paper and placed beneath and transferred to the screen. In the latter process the areas of the screen which are not to be printed are blocked out by the use of wax crayons, shellac, varnish, glue, or lacquer. These materials will act as a stencil in denying the transfer of paint to the printing surface.

In place of the cardboard squeegee one may use a slab of wood, a section of a windshield wiper, or a rubber window cleaner to pull paint across the screen. For more advanced printing a regular squeegee is recommended. It is a simple piece of equipment which features a thick rubber blade inserted into a wooden handle.

A variety of paints can be used in the actual printing. There are many specially prepared silk screen paints; but nu media, genie, tempera, cornstarch paint, as well as textiles, oil, enamel paints and the new plastic lacquers can also be used successfully, provided they are of a creamy or toothpastelike consistency. Choice of paint is dependent upon the type of stencil used and the surface being printed upon. One would not want to use a paint that would dissolve the block-out solution. It is also imperative that the proper solvents be used in the cleaning process.

A Christmas card silk screen made by a nine-year-old using organdy, paper block-out, tempera paint, and a wooden squeegee.

Advanced Silk Screen Printing

Although silk screening is an extraordinarily simple process, it can be a highly skilled craft. As the student becomes more familiar and fascinated with the basic principle of screen printing, he yearns for additional technical knowledge and virtuosity as a means of achieving greater self-expression. The creative student constantly seeks innovations and improvements that are more conducive to his own creative concepts and capabilities. He wants to employ a method that will more precisely communicate his personal convictions and enable him to achieve the proper creative effects.

For the more venturesome student there are the following six challenging techniques, which demand a high degree of craftsmanship and creative control.

Paper block-out

The first and perhaps simplest technique is the paper block-out method which has been mentioned earlier. Almost any kind of lightweight, sturdy paper will do. Newsprint and manila, white drawing, and construction paper are highly recommended, but waxed or oiled papers should be avoided. After the drawing has been decided upon, the appropriate number of stencils are cut or torn. One stencil is cut for each color. The first stencil is then placed in position underneath the screen and attached with a few drops of glue. This will facilitate making a number of prints without danger of the stencil moving out of place. If only a few prints are desired, the stencil may be placed beneath the screen, and the paint run over the silk screen with a squeegee. The plasticity of the paint holds the stencil to the silk. This procedure is followed for each individual stencil.

If water-base paints are used, one may clean the screen with a wet sponge, which will also remove the spots of glue. For other types of paint the appropriate cleaning solvents should be used.

In the hands of creative students, this simple method can result in multicolor prints of unexpected quality. It is not the complexity of the technique but the measure of creativity that counts. This simple method, however, is limited to simple mass forms and does not lend itself to textured or dotted effects.

"Musical Motif," a crayon block-out serigraph by a junior high school student.

Crayon block-out

This method consists of working with crayons directly on the screen beneath which a master drawing or painting has been placed. The drawing is traced and transferred to the screen by the crayon, which fills in the fine mesh of the silk. The resulting print will be a negative image of the original drawing. For a positive print those areas which are not to be printed are filled in with crayon to "block-out" or to prevent the paint from passing through. The master drawing is removed and the desired number of prints are run off. One stencil is required for each desired color. Repairs or changes may be made by touching up the areas to be blocked out. This simple procedure lends itself very well to interesting, textured, vague effects.

Lacquer film block-out

Lacquer stencil film is a specially prepared commercial film composed of a lacquer coating laminated to a sheet of acetate or glassine paper. It is especially recommended for the precise, deliberate work required in poster and textile designs. Pro film and nu film are the two most commonly used. Their transparency permits one to observe the drawing or design underneath while cutting the stencil. The top lacquer layer is cut with considerable care so as not to penetrate the backing paper. The lacquer layer representing the area to be printed is then carefully removed from the acetate sheet.

The stencil is then placed beneath the screen with the lacquer (glossy side) firmly against the silk so that it can be attached. With the use of a soft, absorbent cloth, film-adhering solvent (acetone) is rubbed over the screen a few inches at a time, dissolving the lacquer coating just enough to cause it to adhere to the silk. Do not use a cloth overly saturated with adhering solvent, for too much solvent will cause the film to "burn" or dissolve. Repeat this process from top to bottom until the entire stencil adheres firmly to the silk screen. If, as you remove the backing, the lacquer coating appears to be lifting, stop and repeat the adhering process on that particular area. The stencil is now ready to be printed. Apply the paint with a squeegee as previously described. Separate stencils are required for each color.

Tusche is a liquid plastic that is available with oil or water base. In this particular block-out method, oil tusche is applied to the screen with a brush, a sponge, or by a spatter technique and allowed to dry. A glue solution of 50 per cent glue, 40 per cent water, 8 per cent white vinegar, and 2 per cent glycerine is pulled across the entire screen with a cardboard squeegee. After about a minute the first coat will have dried; another coating of glue is then applied and the excess glue removed. When the glue solution is thoroughly dry it is washed briskly with a soft cloth and a solvent (such as kerosene, turpentine, or benzine) that will dissolve the tusche. The areas to be printed are then freed in order to allow the paint to pass through. Oil-base paints are used in the actual printing. Tusche block-out is one of the methods best suited to the inquisitive high school student with a breadth of interest and an experimental attitude.

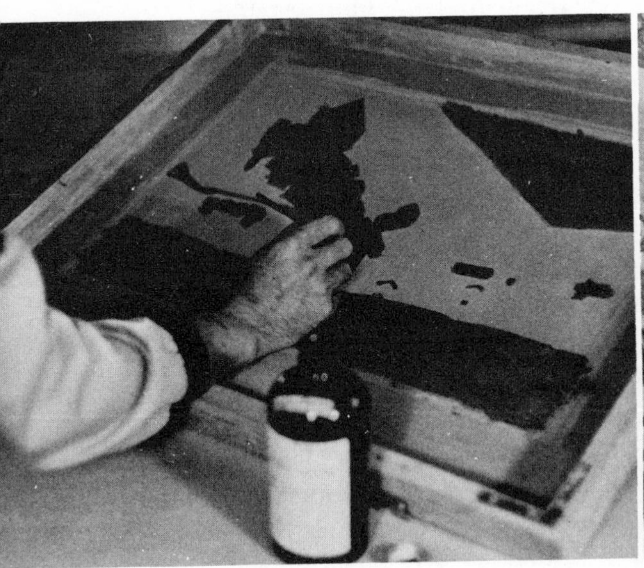

"Crucifixion" by Sister Mary Corita, Immaculate Heart College.

Glue block-out

Glue block-out is the reverse of the tusche method. The entire screen is covered with the glue solution mentioned above, and allowed to dry. The screen is then held to the light and carefully examined for any uncovered areas. These open areas should be retouched with brush and glue. If there are too many pinholes, the entire screen should be covered with a third coating of glue. When the screen is completely blocked out and thoroughly dry, the areas not to be printed are coated with lacquer or shellac, and permitted to dry. The screen is then washed on the inside. A soft cloth and warm water are used to remove the glue from the desired print areas.

An alternate method would be to paint just the areas to be printed with glue solution and to cover the entire screen with lacquer or shellac, and wash out the glue. This is a more positive approach to the glue block-out method. Since this is a lacquer stencil, water-base paints are recommended for the printing.

Above, "Ox in the Forest" (detail) by Ralph Johnstone, University of Southern California. Left, "Crucifixion" (detail) by Sister Mary Corita, Immaculate Heart College. Right, "Ox in the Forest" by Ralph Johnstone, University of Southern California.

Photographic stencil

The photographic stencil is the newest of the printmaker's methods. It is especially important to the commercial designer in silk-screening photographic designs onto textiles and in doing fine lettering on posters. The principle of printing is the same as in the five previous methods; the preparation of the stencil, however, is different. A light-sensitive, gelatin film, laminated to a transparent backing, is placed face to face against a photograph or design, and exposed to light. The exposed gelatin areas are hardened, leaving the protected areas undisturbed. The film is processed in hot water, the unexposed, washed-out areas forming the open stencil areas to be printed. After the stencil adheres to the silk, the transparent backing is removed, making the stencil ready for printing.

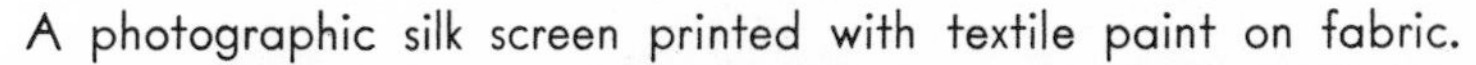
A photographic silk screen printed with textile paint on fabric.

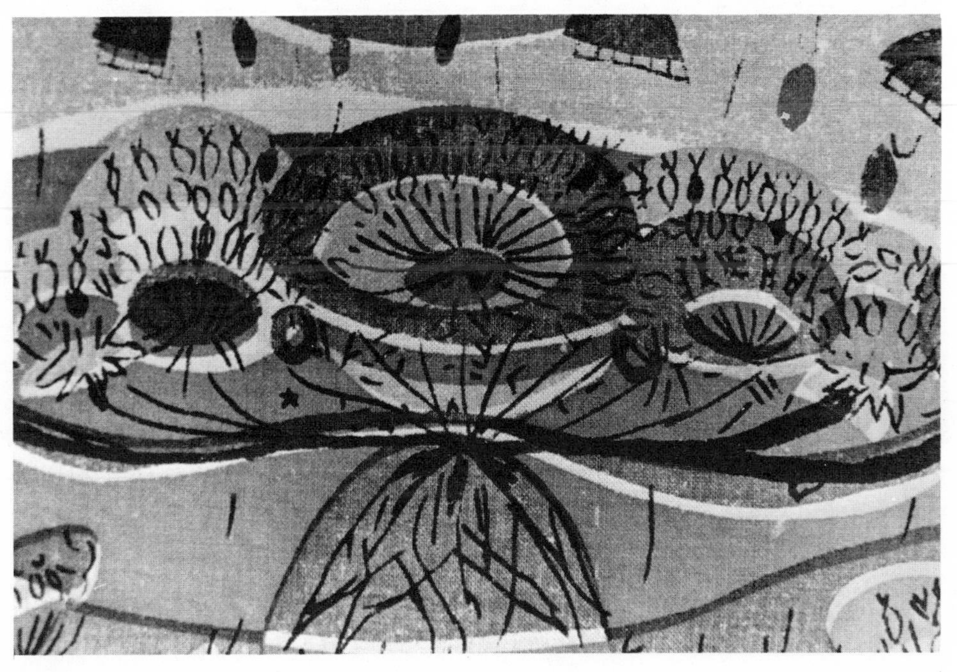

DEKTOL
68°

3

The Photographic Printing Process

Photography, the art of producing images on chemically sensitized paper with the aid of light, is the newest addition to the graphic printing processes. Its possibilities were first realized in 1777, when the Swedish chemist, Karl Scheele, discovered the reaction of light on silver chloride. Its formal introduction, however, did not take place until 1839, when Louise Jacques Mande Daguerre, a French painter who sought to simplify the enormous task of recording the exact likeness of a subject, described his daguerreotype process of making permanent pictures.

For many years thereafter, photography was denied consideration as a division of the fine arts. Since it did not employ a pigment, it was highly literal, and it was not thought adaptable to subjective impressions, photography was not seriously considered to be a genuine printing process. Today, however, it is growing in acceptance and prestige, and is fast becoming recognized as a means of creative expression. A good photograph is as much an aesthetic print as a great lithograph, etching, wood engraving, or serigraph. It has found its rightful place in museums and fine arts galleries.

Photography commonly utilizes a camera loaded with film to record the image. When black-and-white film is developed, it becomes a negative that in some ways might be considered a stencil. This stencil, or negative, may be used to produce many prints. The dark areas of a negative are silver deposits that prevent the light from exposing corresponding areas on the sensitized paper, resulting in white areas in each of the prints. The light or transparent areas of the negative allow the light to pass through, exposing the sensitized paper, and resulting in the imagery of a photograph.

A negative. A positive print.

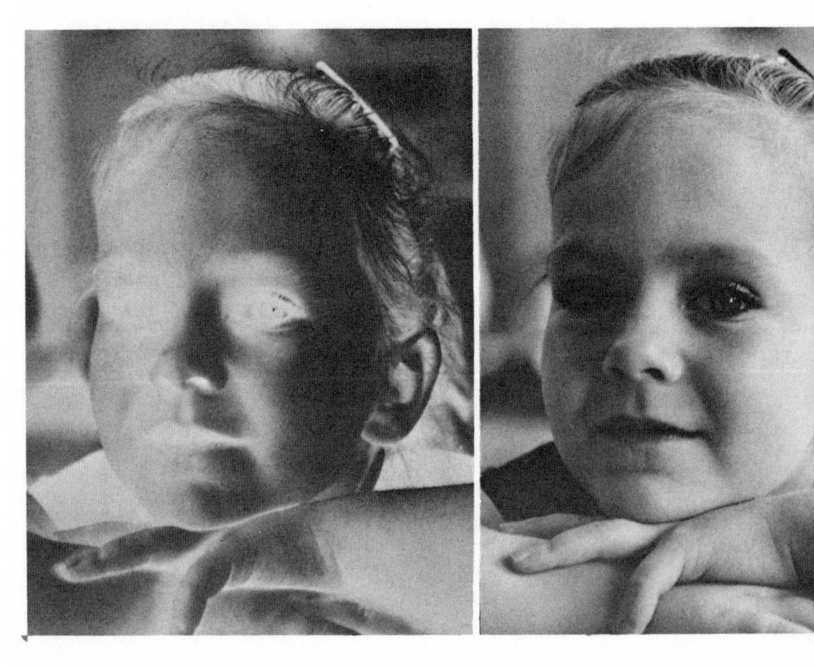

At one time, photographic equipment was cumbersome and expensive, and its use required a high degree of technical virtuosity; today, through constant improvements, the art of photography is within reach of nearly everyone.

The Camera

Kodak Brownie Junior, Six—16.

Perhaps the greatest single innovation in the field of amateur photography was the box camera. It incorporates the basic principle of photography in its simplest form. The camera is merely a box, with an inexpensive lens and shutter at one end and film at the other end. The shutter, lense aperture, and focus are fixed. One has only to load the camera with film, take the pictures, remove the film, and send it out to be processed.

There were many innovations in the cameras that followed. Perhaps one of the most fortunate was the thirty-five millimeter camera. The invention of this miniature camera (which permits the taking of pictures under even poor light conditions) gave the needed momentum to the renaissance of photography after World War II. Constructed with a fast lens * and designed to be fitted with accessory telephoto

* A lens-focal length relationship which allows for maximum exposure in the shortest length of time.

and telescopic lenses, the thirty-five millimeter camera can be used under almost impossible photographic conditions.

Since its inception, the camera has steadily improved and the results are truly amazing and fascinating. There are cameras with ultra-high-speed lenses, and with built-in exposure meters which automatically present the aperture for existing light conditions. With the Polaroid Land camera, the amateur need only push the buttons and count, "a thousand and one—a thousand and two—a thousand and three," and the film is processed right in the camera. One waits only about ten seconds to see the developed picture; if it is unsatisfactory, one aims and shoots again.

Kodak Automatic 35F camera with exposure light meter.

Unfortunately, these miraculous mechanical improvements do not stimulate photography as an art form. On the contrary they usually, unintentionally, restrict the free play of imagination and experimentation and limit the control of one's own creative skills. The camera is undoubtedly the major piece of equipment, but it is nothing more than a means of obtaining a printable negative, which merely allows the artist to reveal his own visual experiences. The artist, not the camera, is still the most important factor in the fine art of photography. In much the same way as in the other four printing processes, the artist, in the way he uses his materials and techniques, is free to express his

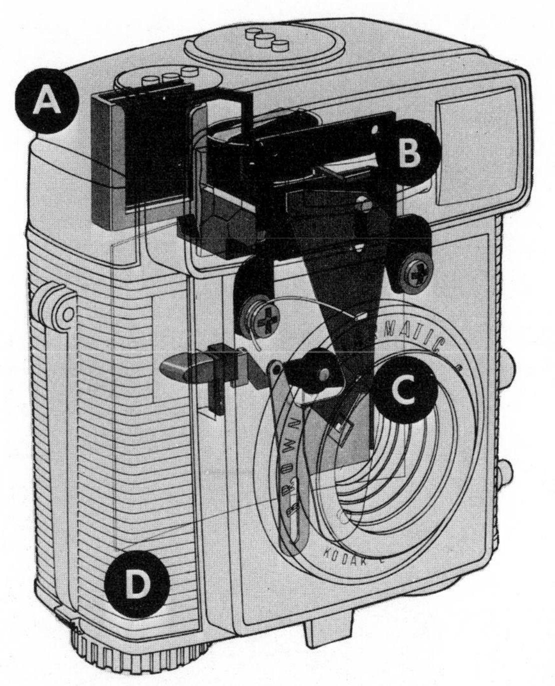

The Brownie Starmatic. The electric eye (A) reads the light and sends an electric current to swing the meter needle (B). When the camera is shot, the lens diaphragm (C) opens only as far as the needle will allow (a tiny opening in brilliant sun, a large opening in shady places). The lens sends just the right amount of light to the film (D) for picture-perfect quality.

own thoughts, ideas, and emotions. The camera is a tool that the artist must master. He excels in spite of the limits of photographic literalism. He interprets the visual world by producing images which the camera is incapable of seeing. He does this by controlling double exposures; by deliberately moving the camera while shooting; by exaggerating with short- or long-focal-length lenses; by arranging the picture composition; by deliberately diffusing the image; and by selecting camera angles.

Not all of the artist's interpretations of a subject involve the camera, however. A variety of interesting effects are created in the darkroom. For example, the control of time and temperature variations, as well as the degree of agitation in developing, will affect the density and contrast of the negative; certain contrast grades in photographic papers will determine the quality of the tone of finished prints; and vignetting, dodging, and cropping can give interest and vitality to what otherwise might have been an ordinary print.

Naturally, any consideration of the photographic process must include a discussion of the equipment and technical means, as well as the creative ends. In an effort not to overshadow our primary concern for the aesthetic values, an attempt will be made to keep the photographic technicalities to a minimum. The wise teacher, however, is well aware that photography as a fine art is the result of the creative ability to express oneself, good camera technique, and a clear understanding of the use of other materials and equipment.

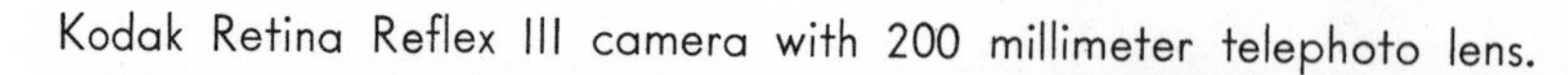

Kodak Retina Reflex III camera with 200 millimeter telephoto lens.

Film

The film in photographic printing is comparable to the stencil in the silk-screening process. It was at one time made of a sheet of glass, coated by hand with a light-sensitive solution containing silver-halide grains, some more sensitive than others. The plate was then exposed and processed, resulting in a heavy, but good, glass negative. As more light came into contact with the plate film, more of the silver grains were exposed, setting up various degrees of density. The areas containing fewer exposed silver grains produced slight degrees of density, while the area covered with a greater number of exposed grains produced greater density.

The modern film of today is a precision-manufactured, thin, flexible, transparent sheet of cellulose nitrate or acetate which functions in much the same way as did glass. The acetate or cellulose nitrate is made by treating cotton with acetic or nitric acid and dissolving it in a chemical solution of ether or alcohol. The solution is distributed evenly on a highly polished cylindrical drum, allowed to dry, and then cut into strips to form the base for the film.

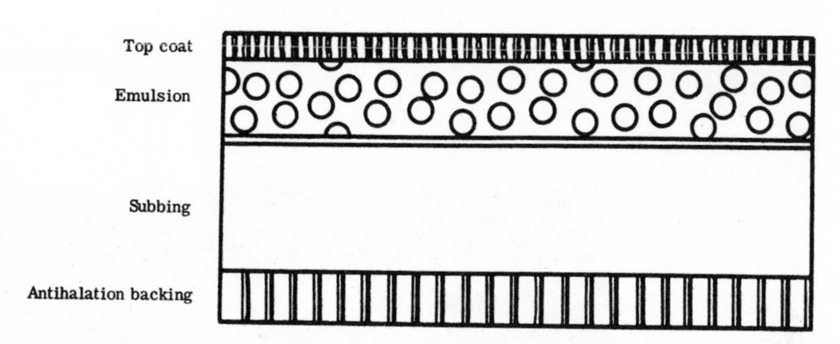

Cross-section drawing of modern film.

This transparent base, which is insensitive to light, is coated with a light-sensitive emulsion of silver bromide. Silver bromide is made by dissolving silver in nitric acid to obtain silver-nitrate crystals, which in turn are added, along with potassium bromide, to a gelatin. Here the bromide and nitrate exchange places. The silver and bromide combine to form the light-sensitive silver-bromide crystals; and the potassium combines with the nitrate and is removed from the gelatin by a washing process. The gelatin is what holds the silver-bromide crystals to the film base during the exposure.

Today's films have an antihalation backing, a dyed gelatin application which absorbs the light rays reflected from the film holder and prevents the halo effect which forms around the bright points of the image.

During the exposure of film, the silver bromide registers an invisible or latent image of its encounter which emerges by turning dark during the developing process. The amount of light striking the film during exposure determines the darkness of the resultant negative right up to the point of maximum darkness-black. On this factor is based the primary principle of photography.

Lighting

Since photography is produced by light, a brief discussion of lighting and its control is of utmost importance. In photography it is imperative that light be considered primarily in terms of the creative effect desired. Lighting can be used to affect the form of the subject and to emphasize the visual mood of the idea. With this in mind we can discuss the source of light. It can either be applied to the subject by artificial means, such as incandescent lamps, or, in the case of natural light, by carefully selecting the time of day and the setting of the subject.

"The Long Shadow" by the author.

Artificial and natural light can be controlled by means of reflectors, screens, and netting. Reflectors can easily be constructed from large sheets of masonite, homosote, plywood, or double-thickness cardboard. These may be painted with either a matte or a glossy-white paint. The matte finish will give a diffused light and unfortunately is effective only at close range. If a more reflective light is desired, one may use sheets of aluminum or crumpled foil. Such natural forms of reflectors as snow, large bodies of water, and sand, when available, can be most effective.

Existing light, especially if intense, may at times be undesirable and can easily be reduced or diffused with background screens, cheesecloth, mosquito netting, or sheets of spun glass. In many cases it is desirable to employ a combination of applied or reflected light and diffused light. Experimentation can result in many interesting effects and can be quite rewarding.

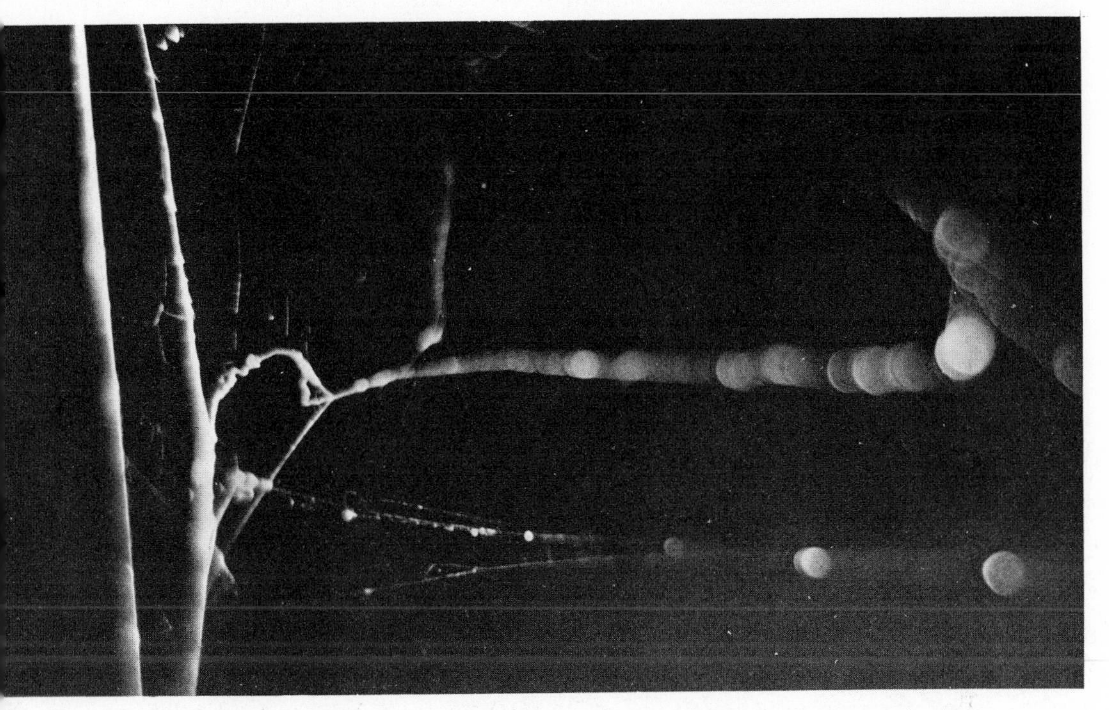

A spider web photographically magnified with extension tubes and shot with the aid of natural light.

Correct Exposure

Before film can be developed, it must be properly exposed to light. If the exposure is incorrect, good resultant prints cannot be expected. Three salient factors must be taken into consideration in film exposure. They are: the intensity of light, which is regulated by the lens aperture—1.4, 2.8, 4, 5.6, 8, and so forth; the length of time the film is exposed, which is regulated by the shutter speed—60, 125, 250, and so forth; and the sensitivity of the film, which is determined by the manufacturer in preparation of the film.

In the simple box camera which had a fixed-focus, single-aperture opening and shutter speed, the film's exposure to light was controlled. The photographer, naturally, was limited to taking pictures in full sunlight. Today, however, with refined precision cameras which incorporate fast lenses and high-speed shutters, with the advent of increased interest in achieving specific effects by deliberate overexposure or underexposure, and with lighting conditions that vary from excellent to poor, some system of calibrating proper exposure must be determined.

The generally recommended devices used in determing the proper exposure are the photocell (or photoelectric meter), the optical meter, and the tables or exposure guides provided by manufacturers of film. The photocell, an instrument which reads foot candles, is most popular. With the photocell's calibrated numbers as a basis, the appropriate aperture and shutter speed setting can be synchronized for a variety of proper exposures, depending on the speed of action and desired depth of field.

There are also fully automatic cameras, which adjust themselves to an amazing range of lighting situations. These built-in electric exposure meters unfortunately do not motivate the photographer's desire for innovation.

Developing the Negative

Exposed film contains the latent image. To produce the latent image on a permanent negative the film must be developed. This must be done in a darkroom lest the film be re-exposed, affecting additional silver grains and destroying the desired image. Safelights permit the photographer to see the various steps he is performing while developing the film.

The film is first placed in a specially prepared "developer" which softens the gelatin, allowing the exposed silver-bromide crystals to be

Infra-red film and a filter were used to obtain the dark sky and strong cloud contrast in this photograph. No filter was used in shooting the photograph on the left on page 75. Panchromatic film and a K-2 filter were used in shooting the photograph on the right on page 75.

transformed into grains of metallic silver. These silver particles are the dark areas that form the imagery of a negative.

After the developing time, which is usually between five and ten minutes, the film is rinsed to remove the developing solution and the unexposed silver crystals. The film is then placed in a fixing solution (hypo) which dissolves all undeveloped silver-bromide crystals from the film surface and permanently fixes the image. After fixation, the developed film is washed for about twenty-five minutes and hung up to dry. A soft viscose sponge or chamois may be used to remove any small droplets of water on the film surface. For a more detailed and workable knowledge of the developing process, the reader is referred to the good books available on photographic techniques listed in the bibliography.

Photographic Paper

The paper used in making photographic prints is specially prepared to withstand the ordeal of water by being first coated with a mixture of barium sulphate and gelatin; this eliminates surface pores and provides a smooth surface for a light-sensitive emulsion containing silver bromide.

There are various photographic printing papers. The most common contain a preponderance of either bromide or chloride in the emulsions. The most basic are the chloro-bromide, bromo-chloride, and bromide emulsions. The straight bromide emulsions have the greatest speed. The chloride is a slow emulsion used mostly for contact prints. Photographic paper comes in a great variety of sizes, weights, colors, surfaces, and contrasts. It varies from extremely thin, to a singleweight, to a thick doubleweight. It comes in (natural) white, degrees of cream, ivory and buff colors, as well as in varying textures, and bright glossy and dull matte surfaces. Most firms produce paper ranging from a low to a high contrast (0 to 5).

The various characteristics of photographic paper can be very confusing for most amateurs. It is, therefore, recommended that the average beginner use a Number 2 paper for all normal photographic uses, including the making of photograms and cliché verre prints. Kodabromide F-2 singleweight paper is highly recommended for use with relatively normal negatives. The letters characterize the Kodak papers and the numbers represent subtypes of different contrast grades. Although Kodabromide F-2 is capable of serving the needs of most school requirements, experimentation is advocated.

Printing the Negative

Now that the pictures have been taken and the film developed, the actual printing takes place. The negative is one's stencil. If it is held up to the light, one can see the imagery in dark and light areas. The dark areas represent the light areas of the original scene and will revert to light areas in the ensuing print; the light areas of the negative are exactly the opposite.

In printing, the negative is placed on a piece of photographic paper; the emulsion sides of the paper and the negative are face to face. Then the two are exposed to light, which passes through the negative and affects the sensitive paper in proportion to the density of the dark areas on the negative. The paper is then placed in a developer solution, an acid stop bath, and a fixing bath, in that order; finally it is washed in clear water. The process differs only slightly from the method of processing the negative. The result is a "contact" print, which is the same size as the negative.

Larger prints may be made by projection. The negative is placed in an enlarger, and the image is focused on the sensitive paper and exposed to light. This is done in a darkroom with the aid of yellow or amber light, in much the same way as contact printing. The photographer, however, has considerably more control over the results, as well as the opportunity of experimenting and making changes.

Since the creative photographer is accustomed to obtaining his own specific effects, it would be presumptuous of the author to attempt to list recommended formulas for developers that would be satisfactory to everyone. The beginner, however, may refer to the recommended formulas in McCoy's book, *Practical Photography,* listed in the bibliography.

The Fine Arts of Photography

Before photography came into existence, the artist searched for and communicated his visual experiences with paint and brush; but in an effort to simplify the tedious task of recording with paint the exact likeness of his subjects—at that time a popular art—he used the camera obscura as an aid in sketching. Unfortunately, this mechanical device, as well as the photographic process that followed, only restricted the artist in his compositions and interpretive expressions. Today, however, a more integral relationship exists between photography and the other arts.

Photography is no longer denied the status of a fine art. In the hands of a creative person it can be a vivid form of communication. A photograph, like any other art form, is a symbol of what the photographer-artist has found interesting, exciting, and meaningful. If his visual experiences have been accompanied by enthusiasm and intense curiosity, his picture is likely to have the vitality of a great work of art.

Picturetaking, like painting, printmaking, or sculpture, should not be done merely to record subject matter. It should, above all, be the result of an individual's exciting response to the experience of seeing with compassion and empathy. A person should take pictures only of things that interest, excite, and move him. The subject, per se, does not matter. It may be people, a landscape, stacked lumber, or an apple. On the other hand, taking a picture with excitement and enthusiasm alone will not guarantee a great print; one must give serious consideration to the principles of art.

"Bather" by Grant Dinsmore, Syracuse University.

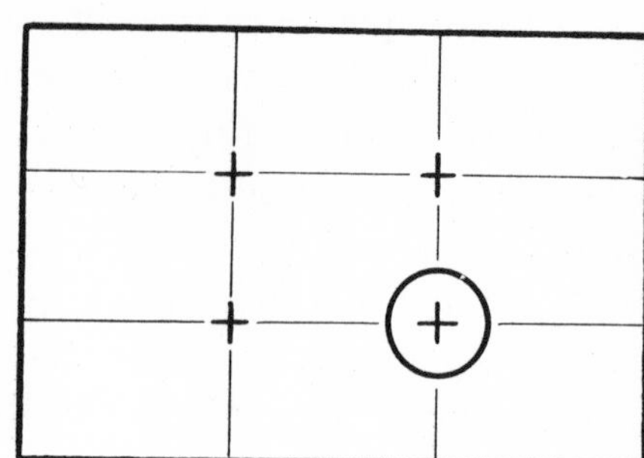

"Discovery" by Grant Dinsmore, Syracuse University. Rule of thirds.

We are not primarily concerned here with the dogma of objective art rules. We shall refer to as "composition" the composite of all visual elements that help make a picture a work of art. It should by all means remain a personal affair. Composition in photography, unlike drawing or painting, must be relevant to the subject matter at hand. It is, therefore, imperative that we select carefully and discriminately from all that we see. Disappointing pictures are usually the result of indifference or untrained seeing.

There are some basic forms and arrangements in visual imagery that are highly pleasing to the eye and can be considered "sure-fire" compositional elements. To be aware of these in composing and cropping prints is definitely an advantage; but to depend upon such compositional elements as ends in themselves can only lead to dull, mechanical, and stereotype pictures.

"Gymnast" by Grant Dinsmore, Syracuse University.

Instead of simply listing, defining, and diagramming basic compositional elements, the author has attempted to illustrate them by using good photographs (horizontal, diagonal, vertical, curves, and large masses). Good photographs invariably reflect compositional elements, but what makes them good is their depiction of real meaning. To compose good, artistic, and meaningful photographic prints one must first train himself in the art of seeing. The world around us is made up of an infinitesimal number of truly beautiful and significant sights that frequently lie hidden from our visual cognition. Only the keenest searching eyes are capable of perceiving this aesthetic treasure. Secondly, in picture-making one must be aware of the unfortunate factors that can ruin a potentially artistic print. Often the picture background camouflages, or distracts from, the main subject. Also, inattention to what the camera is seeing may produce photographs in which subjects walk off the edge of the picture, and telephone poles grow out of people's heads; one's photos may become populated by noseless or headless men and women, victims of obscurant foreground objects.

The only golden rule that can be applied effectively to picture-making is to "try it on the eye." Arrange the compositional elements so that in the resulting print they reveal what you intended to convey. If it looks right to you, if it says what you want it to say, it is most likely that you have a good picture.

"Flying South" by Grant Dinsmore, Syracuse University.

The few rules-of-thumb which follow may be taken into consideration when photographing pictures, but they must be considered only as possible means to ends. Use the golden rectangle or the "rule of thirds," especially in action shots; plan the horizon line so that it falls below or above the center of the paper; make converging lines or forms of contradiction reveal something of interest at the point of contact; allow the background to work for you by using forms of transition to order movement, or by leading the eye to the points of greatest interest; use vertical or horizontal compositions to emphasize tallness or broadness.

There are many more rules-of-thumb that may be learned as you delve into photography. The most important thing to keep in mind, however, is to select and arrange compositional elements carefully so that they make sense, set the mood of your ideas, and reveal the emotions you wish to convey. To do this, of course, is not easy. But, fortunately, what cannot be accomplished with the camera lens in photographing the subject can frequently be corrected in proper cropping.

All one needs for cropping is a pair of "L"-shaped pieces of cardboard. The "L"-shaped cardboards are laid over the photograph and moved about. They are kept at right angles to each other and manipulated until a pleasing composition is obtained.

Photograms

Whereas the photographic process that has been discussed commonly uses a camera to record imagery on a negative, there are other methods of photographic printing that do not require the use of a lens or camera. The most common is the printing of photograms. Making photograms is a very simple process which requires only one's imagination, a darkened room, photographic paper, a 40- or 60-watt electric light bulb, flat opaque objects, and a few chemicals in the form of liquid or crystals ready to be dissolved in water. The chemicals can be purchased from any photography shop.

Such objects, which may be found around the house or classroom, are at first assembled in interesting design patterns on the sensitive paper and exposed to light. The exposed paper is then developed and fixed in the manner described in the section on printing the negative.

The photogram seen here was made by a seventh-grade student. The design was created by placing string, paint, pieces of opaque paper, a piece of cellophane, and a hair curler on a sheet of glass. The glass was then carried into the darkened supply room and placed on a sheet of singleweight Kodabromide F-2 paper, and exposed to the light of a desk lamp for four seconds. The paper was immediately immersed in a developer (Dektol) at 68° F. for a minute, placed in water for a few seconds, then put in fixing solution for twenty minutes, and finally washed in running water.

For most effective photograms, arrange three trays so that they can be easily used from one position. In the first tray place the developer, in the second tray the stop bath (which is 1½ ounces of 28 per cent acetic acid and 32 ounces of water, cooled to 68° F.), and in the

Cut paper and bits of nature, with the aid of single weight Kodabromide F-2 photographic paper and regular developing solutions, were used to create the above photograms.

third tray place the fixing bath at the same temperature. The photographic paper should then be slipped—not dropped—into the developer so that the entire sheet is submerged. It should be agitated by gently rocking the tray from time to time for one minute. The print should then be placed in a stop bath, rinsed for ten to fifteen seconds, and placed in the hypo fixing bath for twenty minutes, after which it is washed in running water for approximately an hour. The finished prints are dried by being placed between photographic printing blotters or by being rolled in clean, absorbent cloth or paper.

Students who have never created photograms are usually very enthusiastic about this new process. They will eagerly gather interesting materials to use for their designs. Their initial reaction is one of intrigue and curiosity. In an effort to explore the new medium, their first attempts may result in a conglomeration of materials poorly arranged and hastily printed, but as the novelty wears off the student will concentrate on producing more interesting and various modifications.

The "Dancing Children" photogram was created by using torn construction paper for the foreground figures. Waxed paper was used for the figures in the background, as well as the mountains and the darker, transparent circles. The white opaque circles were made with circles punched from construction paper.

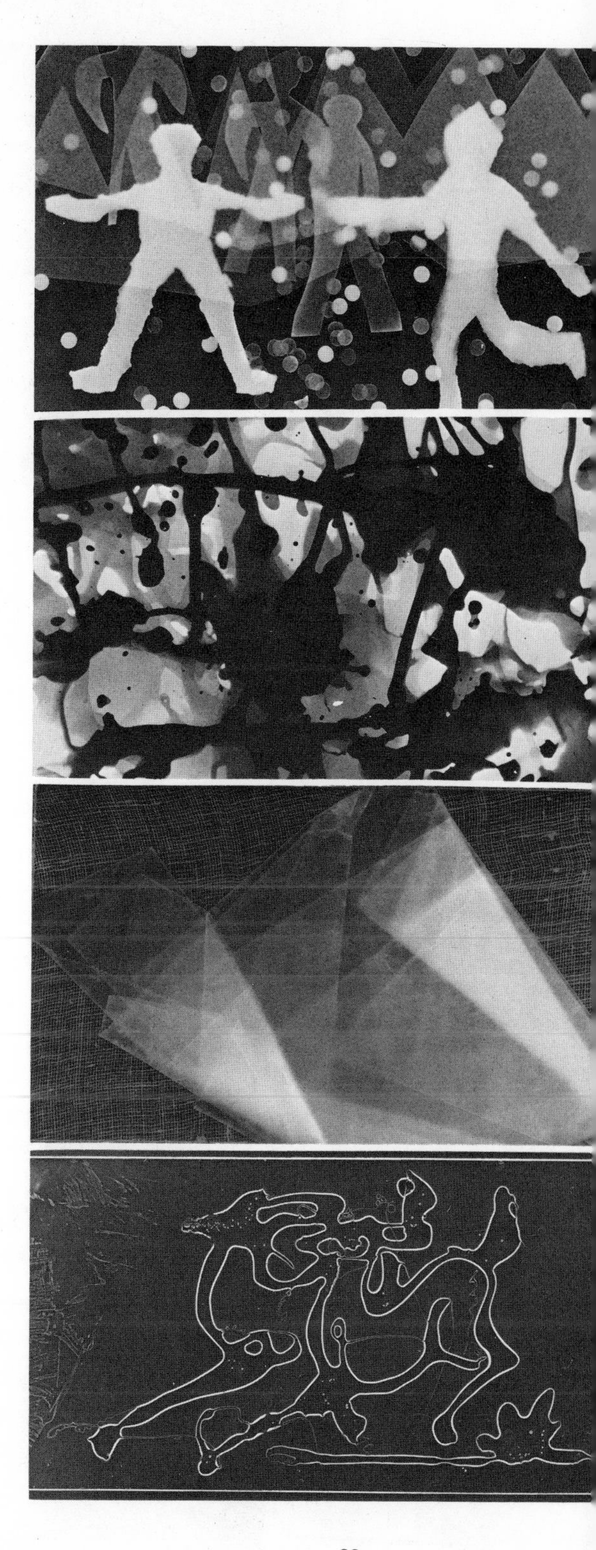

This interesting photogram was made by applying hypo solution to photographic paper, exposing it to light for a few seconds, and then processing it in the usual manner.

The use of a great variety of opaque, translucent, and transparent materials may be used in creating photograms. The results (right) of an experiment reveal the use of waxed paper and cheese cloth. Note the overlapping of transparencies.

The deer photogram was created by squeezing rubber cement on a sheet of glass and developing. Notice how the outer edge of the rubber cement on the piece of glass results in a strong white line effect.

Those who wish to produce more than the simple black-and-white prints may attempt different tonalities of gray by using various paints, inks, and lacquers; colored cellophane and open-textured materials such as hair and corsage netting; powders sprinkled on the glass plate; and many other materials and techniques. The more mature students, who have a better understanding of the concept, will experiment with a variety of transparent materials and devise many interesting methods of making photograms of their own. They may attempt painting on glass, plexiglas, clear plastic, or cellophane with opaque and/or transparent paints or inks. The result will be a white picture on a black background. The print shown of the horse and buggy was created by using a sheet of cellophane. Water that was accidentally splashed on the cellophane produced the gray tones, adding greater interest.

The photograms below are the result of experiments with special light sources. An all-purpose jackknife was used to create the photogram on the left. Fish netting and the seeds of a milk weed were used to create the interesting photogram on the right.

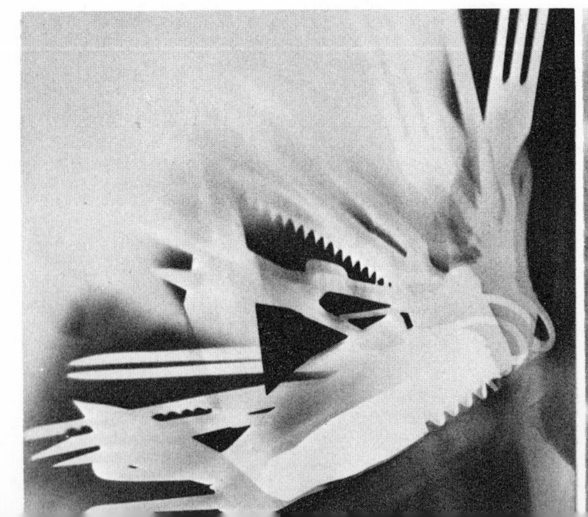

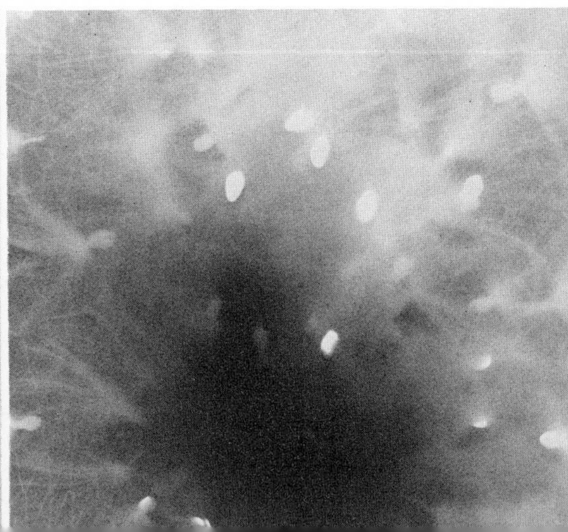

Cliche Verre

An alternate method would be to paint the entire surface of the glass and then to scratch away the design areas. This will produce a design in black, on a white background. This procedure of scratching opaque paint from glass was very popular with the French impressionists, who referred to it as "cliché verre." The results, if executed by a craftsman with a sharp instrument, can resemble a dry-point print.

The same effects may be obtained by scratching fine lines into the emulsion side of overexposed negatives. Since the emulsion of the negative is very thin and flexible, it is easily scratched. This method is so easy that it can be handled without too much difficulty, even by the youngest of students. Should any errors be made, they can easily be corrected by recoating the negative with paint or lacquer.

The photogram at right was produced by scratching through a thick layer of India ink which had been applied to a sheet of plexiglas and left to dry. Any sharp instrument may be used to scratch. The student who created this cliché verre used a regular ink pen.

Experimental Photography

The average art teacher is seldom acquainted with the experimental aspects of the photographic process. Art teachers familiar with photography may have made photograms by placing opaque and translucent materials on photographic paper, briefly exposing it to light, and then printing it; but very few have experienced the montage technique, printing from colored slides, the solarization of negatives (overexposure), and reticulation (immersion of film in very hot water, causing the silver grains to clump and the film emulsion to wrinkle) of negatives. Still fewer teachers have experimented with the camera itself, or with the different types of film emulsion, developers, photographic paper, and lighting effects. Henry W. Ray, to whom we are indebted for his remarks on montage, color transparencies, and solarization, in his article on "Experimental and Creative Photography," * provides us with a challenge for more comprehensive experimentation.

Henry Ray used a camera rather than a photogram technique to create this unusual montage. It is classified as experimental photography.

The camera may be used to create unusual montages. The example shown was made by combining cutout figures with an unusual background. In this example, an old film can which was burned with trash developed an unusual surface of light and dark areas, shapes and texture. Upon this background cutout figures were superimposed and a photograph was taken. The resultant print, combining the images, has a mystic quality and represents the maker's vision. There are no limits other than those of the imagination and sensitivity of the individual with the camera.

* Henry W. Ray, "Experimental and Creative Photography," *Art Education Bulletin,* The Eastern Arts Association, XIX, No. 5 (June, 1962), pp. 25–32.

"The River Boat" by Ron Burke was produced by applying an opaque paint to a sheet of glass, placing it over a piece of photographic paper, exposing it to light, and processing it. The result is the opposite of a cliché verre. The image produced is white on black.

Positive color transparencies were used as "negatives" in the enlarger to produce these photograms. Color transparencies are projected on enlarging paper, resulting in "negative" prints. The gray values are the reverse of the typical photographic print. Since enlarging paper is not sensitive to red or orange light, it is best to use slides that do not have much red or orange subject matter. A "soft" enlarging paper such as Kodabromide contrast grade number one will produce the widest range of gray tones. A "hard" paper such as Kodabromide contrasts grade number five will result in a print with a narrow range of gray tones.

The photograms below were made by using a kodachrome slide as a negative. Such photograms are, in reality, negatives of the slides used.

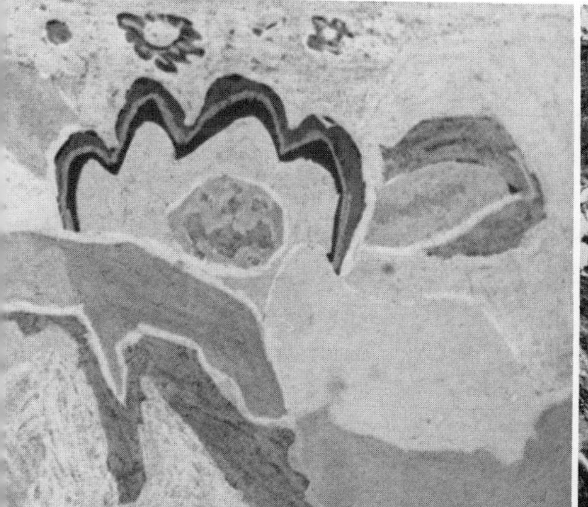

Solarized negatives like the one shown here may be printed on film and the resulting positive used to produce interesting photographic prints.

The solarization process involves little more than exposing the negative very briefly to light during development. Results can never be predicted. Sometimes a complete reversal occurs, in which case the resulting print is itself a negative image. The example shown was originally exposed on Eastman Tri-X in Eastman's Dektol developer diluted in the ratio of one part stock developer to one part water. After approximately four minutes' development in total darkness, the negative was exposed to light—in this case, a simple flashlight—for a second or two, after which development was continued for another two minutes. (Developer solution was in temperature range of 65–68° F.) The negative was then rinsed in a weak acetic acid bath, fixed, washed, and dried in the usual manner.

Sheet films are easiest to experiment with. Results will vary with different film types; Eastman's Pantomic-X, for instance, will give results different from another type of sheet film. For experiments such as these, films that are out of date and useless for general photography can be used. The cost of outdated film is generally a fraction of the cost of current film.

Blueprinting

Blueprints may be made in much the same way as photograms. Miscellaneous opaque and transparent objects are placed on blueprint or velite paper in the desired composition and exposed to light. Conventional blueprint paper, however, has the advantage of being relatively inexpensive, requires no chemicals in the processing, and demands very little technical skill. Although a sunlamp is recommended for the best results, a desk lamp with a 60-watt bulb, or even sunlight is satisfactory. If velite is used, take the precaution of placing the desk lamp at least five or six feet from the paper.

The length of exposure is best determined by experimentation. The paper is usually left until it becomes discolored; and this, of course, is dependent upon the source of light. After the paper has been exposed, it is placed in water for about ten minutes, and finally set to dry. If a deeper and more vivid blue is desired, the paper may be washed in the usual way and then placed in a solution of one part potassium alum and twenty parts water, after which it is again washed in clean water and dried. Hydrogen peroxide may be used instead of potassium alum. The blueprint process offers a simple printing experience and may be fascinating to the very young. However, the possibilities of any creative challenge are limited; therefore, little is offered the more advanced students.

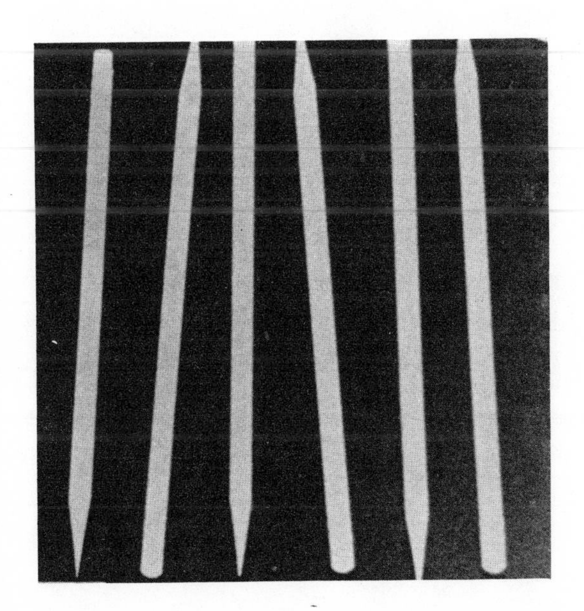

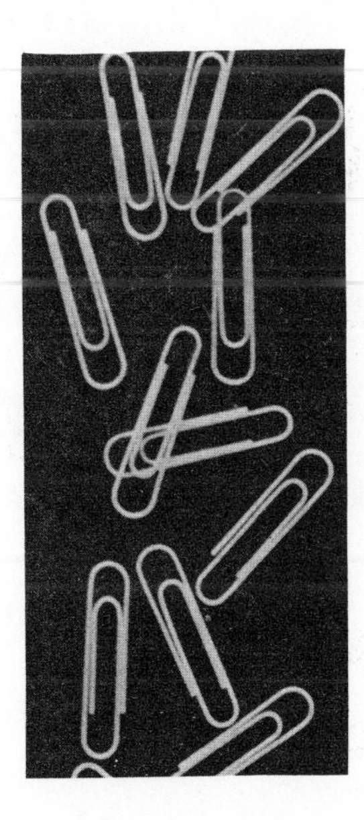

4

The Planographic Printing Process

Planography, more commonly known as lithography, is a process of printing from a flat, smooth surface upon which the printing and nonprinting areas are approximately the same level. These areas are distinguished only by the thickness of the substance applied, which is usually a medium consisting of fatty acids such as wax, resin, or tallow plus a carbon or charcoal pigment. This medium is better known to us as a lithographic pencil or crayon. The process of lithography was first introduced in 1796 by Aloys Senefelder, who noticed that certain stones had an affinity for both oil and water. He drew on a stone, using a greasy substance; when the stone was dampened, the water was repelled from the greasy area. Then, attempting to ink this entire stone with an oil-base pigment, Senefelder discovered that the pigment adhered only to the greasy area; the damp parts of the stone would not absorb the oily pigment. When he placed a sheet of paper against the stone, the pigment was transferred to the paper.

The following simple experiment illustrates the antagonism of oil and water and serves as a preliminary step in understanding the basic principle of lithography. First, a drawing is made on paper with wax crayons, applying a sufficient amount of wax to repel a water paint. The entire sheet of paper is then brushed over with a coating of a dark-colored, water-base paint. Begin at the top of the paper and brush across lightly with a brush charged with paint, overlapping each previous stroke until the bottom is reached. Do not scrub the paint into the colored wax. Notice that the paint is repelled by the wax and adheres only to the exposed paper. This drawing is called a "crayon-resist." If the paint is not repelled, it may be that sufficient wax has not been applied or that the paint was too thick. The paint should be of a light, creamy consistency. It is best to allow the students to create their own crayon-resist drawing, since, for those who have actually experienced this principle, the antagonism of oil or wax and water becomes more meaningful. This drawing, of course, is not a lithograph. In fact it is based on the reverse of the principle of lithography. There is no transfer of imagery and no actual printing. The drawing merely serves to point out that oil-base pigments resist water. This, in reality, is the basic principle of lithography.

Lithography, until now, has always been considered an inappropriate medium for the public school art programs. High school students, and certainly elementary school children, have been deprived of its exciting experiences because of formidable obstacles: lithography's costly and cumbersome equipment; the complexity of a procedure that demands deliberate care; the enormous output of strenuous labor; and the need for considerable time in graining, etching, and washing the stone. Lithography, however, can be created by the simplest means. There are a number of reproductive techniques, any one of which, although not literally a lithographic process, has some relation to lithography. These simple experimental methods of reproduction can easily be experienced by young children and are ideal for introducing them to the planographic printing process.

A rubbing created by placing the forms of a baseball image cut from cardboard upon a flat surface, covering it with a sheet of light-weight paper, and rubbing it on the top side with a crayon.

Rubbings

Shortly after the invention of paper, the reproductive techniques for making stone rubbings became a popular art. This was the Chinese method of making impressions of the designs and inscriptions carved into the flat stone surfaces of the large burial storage boxes and on the mass-produced molded bricks used in the construction of tombs. The process was a relatively simple one. A dampened sheet of rice paper was pressed against relief sculpture or design and forced into the lower recesses. With the paper still firmly pressed against the design, ink was applied with the aid of a flat and firm pad. By rubbing on top of the paper, the reversal of the image which occurs in so many printing techniques is avoided.

"Adirondack" by Margaret Jennison, Syracuse University.

Rubbings are not considered legitimate lithographs, but they do have the distinct appearance of a lithographic print. "Relief printing" is probably the most descriptive name for this process. The technique is so simple that it can easily be executed by most children. They may even be encouraged to create their own designs by placing forms of cut cardboard, coins, screen, and string in a composition upon a flat surface and covering it with a piece of paper. Dampening the paper, as the early Chinese did, is not necessary. After being placed on the design, the paper is lightly rolled with an inked brayer. By varying the pressure on the brayer as it is rolled across the different areas, tonal effects can be controlled. In addition to ink, one may rub crayon, chalk, or charcoal across the prepared surface. A combination of media may be tried for unique and unusual effects. Students should be encouraged to discover for themselves untried ways of exploiting this ancient art of "stone rubbing."

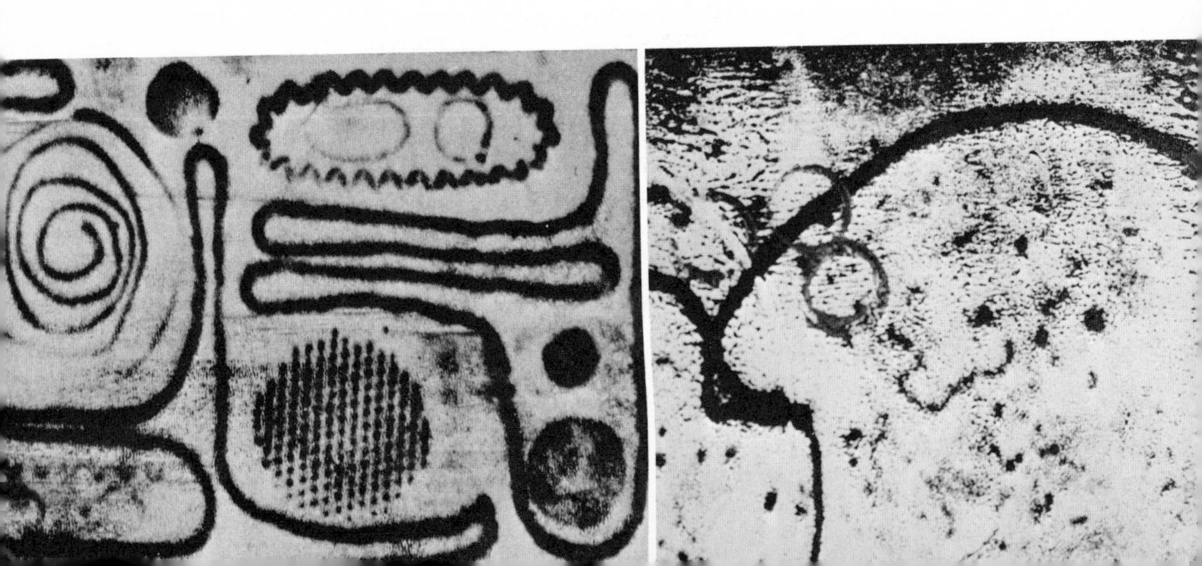

Monoprints

A monoprint is an impression taken from a painting done on a piece of glass, metal, or other hard, nonabsorbent, smooth surface. Although only a single print can usually be made from one painting, this process involves transferring an image from one surface to another and, therefore, can be classified as a print. The technique can be extremely simple, needing very little time; or it can be complex, requiring a number of colored, slow-drying pigments, considerable time, and technical skill. Some form of tractable pigment, generally paste or oil-base paint, is spread evenly over the entire surface of a sheet of glass or masonite with the hands, a brush, or a brayer. The image is then incised into the paint, exposing the surface of the plate. The impressions may be made with almost any instrument capable of making a mark in the paint. While the paint is still wet, a sheet of paper is laid over it and rubbed gently on the back. The print paper may then be pulled or peeled away. The result will be what is referred to as a white-line print. The color effect may be reversed by printing light-colored paints on dark-colored ground paper.

Finger paint monotypes are most appropriate for the very young. A thick layer of finger paint is spread evenly over the surface of a sheet of masonite or plate glass and incised with the aid of both dull and sharp instruments. The children may use tongue depressors, pencils, erasers, pieces of cardboard and wood, and swab sticks. Fingers, of course, are the most plausible means. Monoprints of one color are extremely easy to make and require very little time. A young child executes two and sometimes three different prints in a single period. It is an excellent way of teaching that most printing processes print the image in reverse. Children can also learn about the effects of color and texture and their relationship on a print. More advanced children may attempt to incorporate two, or even three, separate colors on the ground.

Another method of monoprinting with finger paints involves the act of drawing more directly than the process just described. The surface plate is coated with finger paint in the usual manner, but in-

stead of making an intaglio impression, a sheet of thin paper is placed over the paint and the image is then drawn directly on the ground paper from the top. The rubbing step which normally precedes the pulling of the print is omitted. When the print is pulled, the result will still be a reverse image, but it will be a dark-line print on a white ground with impressed light tones of the paint used to cover the plate. These tonal impressions may be controlled by varying pressure on the different areas of the final ground before it is pulled.

Monoprints may also be produced in full color. The image is meticulously painted on the surface plate with slow-drying paints. It is covered in the usual manner and gently rubbed with the bowl of a spoon

"Arearea No Varua Ino" by Paul Gauguin, National Gallery of Art, Washington, D.C. (Rosenwald Collection).

or rolled with a clean brayer. Advanced students may try blending the paints lightly with a spatula, tongue depressor, or brayer; or they may press screen, burlap, or various textured materials against the printing surface and remove them, leaving the impression to register later on the final ground. These simple techniques are cogent evidence that the approach to monoprinting can be a challenge for any high school student.

There are a number of inexpensive materials that may be recommended for use in making monoprints. Each material lends itself to a certain range of experimental research. The best pigments to use with the young children are the washable, water-base pigments such as the commercial, all-purpose nu media and genie paints, as well as finger paint and home-made cornstarch and flour paste paints. The older children may use the slow-drying water colors and oil-base paints.

A drawing may be done on the surface of the plate with an assortment of implements. Brushing, spraying, dabbing, blotting, rubbing, and pressing, plus many other forms of attack that you will undoubtedly discover as you experiment, produce interesting effects. New effects may also be discovered by combining paints of different bases, such as oil and watercolor, or adding vaseline to tempera paint.

Any of the all-purpose, inexpensive art papers may be used. Newsprint, construction paper, manila, and drawing paper are but a few. One may even experiment with printing on wood, cellophane, and various fabrics; metallic-coated, textured, or rice paper may also be used. These materials may add to the already almost numberless varieties of effects and qualities.

Although a monoprint commonly originates from a smooth surface such as a sheet of glass or masonite, the quality of the resulting print may be entirely changed if wood, stone, plaster, or cloth is used. There is probably no end to the materials which can be used in experimentation. Fathoming the reaches of one's imagination in the search for specific effects stimulates the mind's growth. For some people, the resulting prints may serve only as a springboard for departure from printing entirely; henceforth only drawing or painting into the print surface may satisfy them. Carrying forward an idea and seeking the best means for its expression, whether it be a print, collage, or a complete innovation, can be a very profitable venture. Though the purist may complain that it is an illegitimate approach to printmaking, we must remember that our objective is to deal with rules not for their own sake but rather for the sake of discovery and greater aesthetic development.

As we have previously stated, the actual lithographic process has had a reputation of being a somewhat mysterious process involving almost magical occurrences and expensive materials and machinery. It is true that there is much more involved in making a lithograph than there is in making simple monoprints. There is, however, a very simple means of creating a lithographic print from a sheet of specially prepared litho sketchmaster paper.

Simple Paper Lithography

Lithographic prints can now be made from a lithographic coated paper surface. The drawing is made with litho-crayon, pencil, and/or tusche. Once the drawing is complete, the plate is desensitized with lithographic plate solution, inked, and printed. The laborious task of graining, etching, and washing the cumbersome stone is dispensed with. The four basic steps to "litho-sketch" are discussed in sufficient detail to permit the nonprofessional a successful experience in making a lithographic print. The materials required are: a piece of glass or masonite; a soft rubber brayer; a sheet of sketchmaster plate; stiff cardboard; a bottle of rubber cement; lithographic crayons, pencils, and/or tusche; lithographic plate solution; cotton swabs; printer's ink; and a wringer or simple, roller-type press.

The drawing

A sheet of sketchmaster plate is glued to a stiff, smooth piece of cardboard and cut to the desired size. The drawing is then created with a variety of lithographic pencils, crayons, and tusche. Avoid getting finger prints on the sensitized surface of the printing plate, because the hands have a natural oil to which printer's ink reacts just as it does to the lithographic crayons. The best pencils to begin with are numbers four and five. If tusche is being used it should be of a liquid consistency to insure a free flow in the drawing. If tones of gray are desired, the tusche may be thinned with distilled water. The plate should be thoroughly dry before the desensitizing solution is applied.

The desensitizing

The drawing is prepared for inking by being desensitized with a coating of lithographic plate solution. Saturate a cotton applicator with the solution and moisten the entire plate's surface. Do not permit the applicator to drip. Squeeze out any excess solution before starting to desensitize the litho sketchmaster plate. Experiment to discover the right amount of plate solution needed. Too much solution will tend to retard the printer's ink and keep it from being deposited; too little solution will not protect the nonprinting areas from being charged with ink, thus preventing the desired effects.

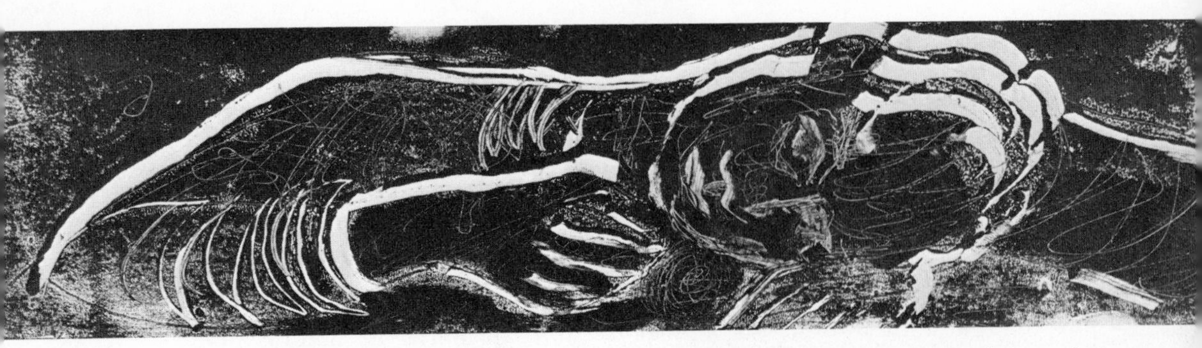

Undesirable spots or excessive inking may be removed by wiping the area with plate solution. Stubborn areas can be loosened with an ink eraser and wiped clean with plate solution. One should always use a clean applicator to prevent redeposits of ink where they are not wanted. The printing plate should be desensitized before each inking.

The inking

An oil-base printer's ink is squeezed from the tube onto a glass plate, or some other nonabsorbent smooth surface, and spread evenly with a brayer until it becomes tacky. Only lithographic inks are recommended. The water block-printing inks are not satisfactory on litho sketchmaster plates. The initial plate should be inked two or three times for a good print. The first print will be rather light. It usually takes three or four proofs before a plate can build up a full charge of ink. To prevent emulsification, the brayer should be rolled lightly over a sheet of cardboard prior to charging it on the inking pad. This will remove any excessive plate solution picked up by the roller from the plate.

The printing

The actual printing is accomplished by the application of pressure. A clean sheet of paper is carefully placed over the inked plate. The paper should be slightly larger than the plate. It need not be dampened. A printer's blotter or a piece of clean cardboard is placed on top of the print paper to protect it, and the three pieces are carefully run through a wringer or roller press. The ordinary, hand-turned washing machine wringer will give quite satisfactory results. Good results have also been obtained by using the spoon method of applying pressure. Lithographic prints may be made on almost any kind of paper. Newsprint, manila, drawing paper, or construction paper will give excellent results. The better-quality papers naturally will give better-quality prints.

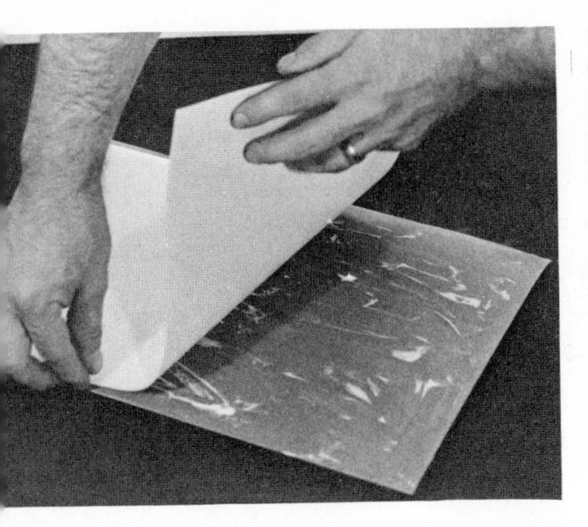

Mounting the paper.

Creating the image.

Desensitizing the plate.

Inking the plate.

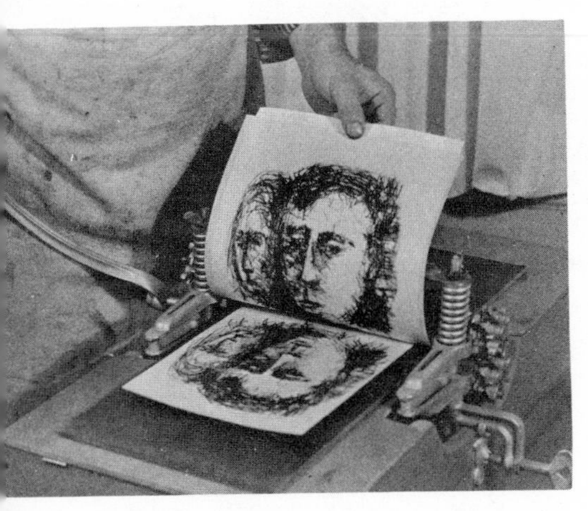

Applying the pressure.

Preserving the plate.

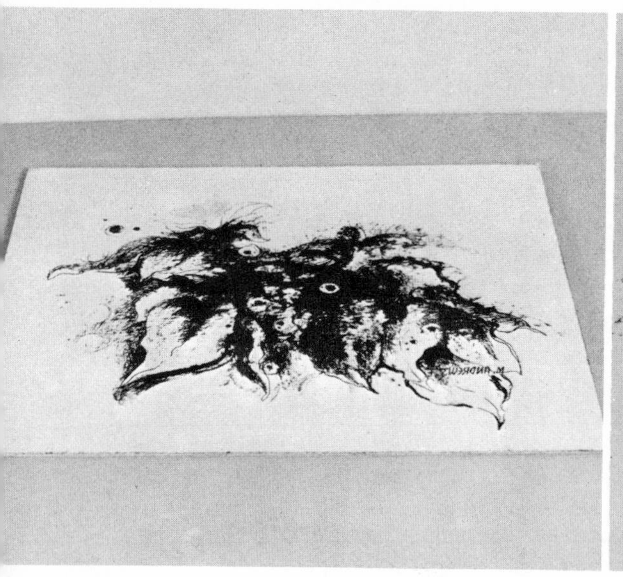

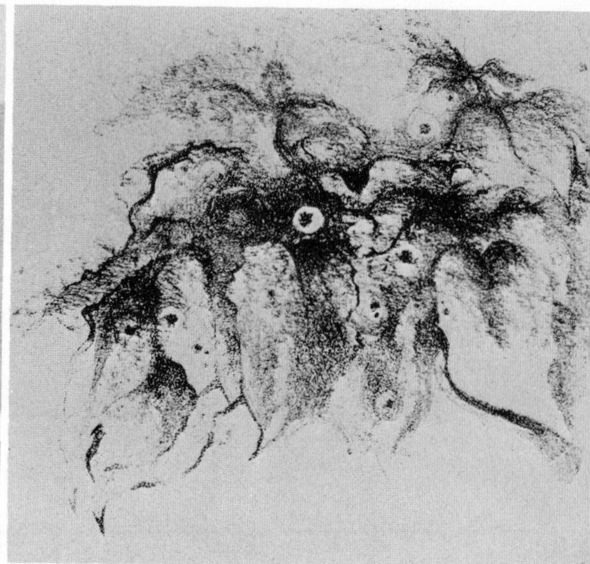

At left is a sketchmaster paper glued to a sheet of smooth illustration board. Textured board, however, may be used for special effects. The drawing was made with a number four lithographic pencil. At right is the resultant print. Sketchmaster prints can be made in more than one color.

Litho-sketch is a product of Anthony Ensink Company. The materials can be purchased from Sax-Arts and Crafts, Milwaukee, Wisconsin.

"Doves" by Michelle Ryan, Syracuse University.

Stone Lithography

Although specially coated paper and metal plates with grained surfaces may be used successfully in lithographic printing, lithography, as the term implies (litho = stone, graphy = to write), is fundamentally a stone printing process. The traditional process of "stone printing" provides a much greater and more subtle range of possibilities than do paper and metal plates and should, therefore, be made available to the more advanced students. With the use of fine-grained Bavarian limestone, which is chiefly quarried near Soenhofen, the students can be given the opportunity to experience the richness of tonal qualities, the interplay of textures, and the definition of form.

Lithography was once considered too difficult and demanding a procedure for high school students. It required too much time and patience to be considered practical. Today, however, it is no longer necessary to use the heavy, cumbersome stones and the complex, prohibitively expensive handpress. Several simple and compact portable printing presses of the roller type are adaptable for printing lithography from a stone cradle in a chase. Such presses have put stone lithography within the reach of every aesthetically minded high school student.

"Tomah Rock" by Santo Zingale, University of Wisconsin.

The Laszlo printmaker's press illustrated here is a portable press which can be clamped to the edge of any sturdy table. The press is set by adjusting screws. There are two rollers. The upper roller has a steel core covered with high-density rubber and is rotated by means of three convenient arms. The lower roller is made of steel and rotates on precision roller bearings. The press is equipped with two interchangeable beds, making it equally adaptable to relief and intaglio printing.

The initial cost of setting up a lithography workshop is much less than that required for many other subject areas of a progressive high school, and the cost of maintenance and supplies makes it one of the least expensive.

The values derived from printing with stone more than compensate for the time, effort, and cost involved in the process. It is a unique experience which promotes the study of line and form, reveals the conception of chiaroscuro, and enriches the appreciation of the graphic arts.

A print from stone by a college student.

The Laszlo portable press.

The principle of making a lithograph from stone is basically the same as for paper lithography. There are, however, a few additional steps which we shall discuss in detail for those who may wish to do a lithograph with stone.

Graining the stone

Only the stones that have been used and still possess old drawings need be grained. New stones have a clean surface and, therefore, do not need graining. Wet the stone to be grained with water and then sprinkle with a tablespoon of carborundum. Spread the carborundum evenly over the entire surface of the stone, place a slightly smaller slab of smooth limestone on top of the one being grained, and, with a rotating motion, grind the image off the stone to be used in the printing. By grinding with a consistent pressure over the entire surface of the stone, and at times putting the top stone on the bottom, unevenness in the stone surface may be prevented. From time to time the muck formed by the abrasive, water, removed particles of the limestone, and grease will make grinding difficult. When this happens, wash the stones and start with clean water and additional carborundum. Continue the process, adding the abrasive and water until the entire drawing is removed.

"Encounter #1" by Morton Kaish, New York City.

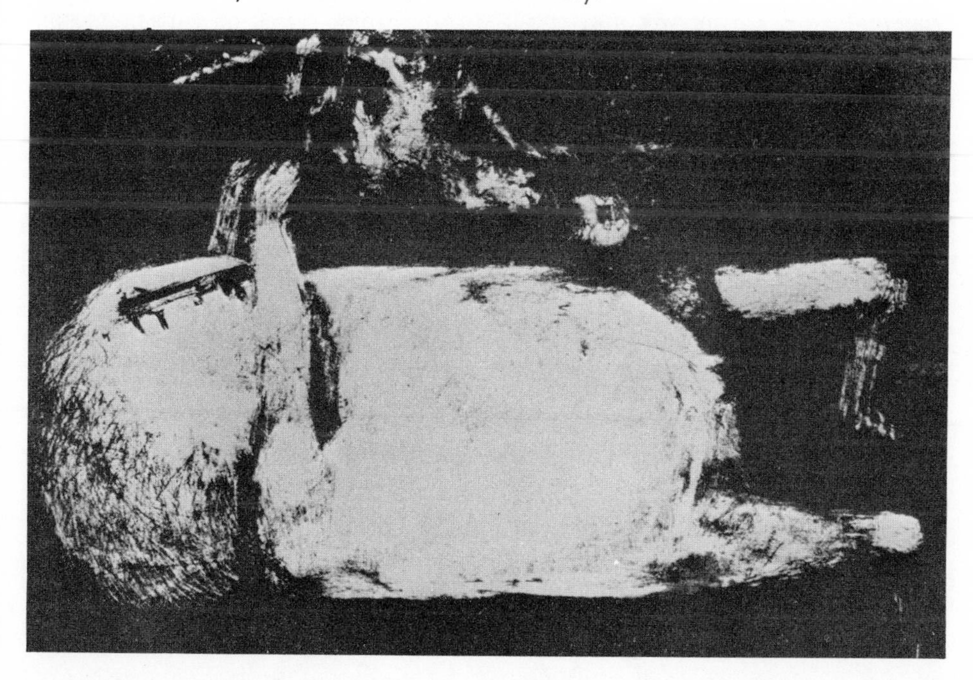

The final grinding should be done with fine carborundum to assure a smooth drawing surface. When finished, the top stone is carefully slid off the bottom stone, and both stones are thoroughly washed and dried. The new image may now be drawn on either stone. Stones that are not immediately used should be covered with a sheet of newsprint to protect the printing surface from dust and finger smudges.

Drawing the image

The created image should, by all means, be an autobiography of the printmaker's visions, impressions, and interpretations. The range of personal expression is limited only by the imagination of the individual manipulating the medium. This aesthetic aspect cannot be overemphasized, regardless of the age level of the printmaker.

We are at present, however, interested primarily in the fundamentals of imposing or transposing the image to the stone. If the image is to be imposed, or drawn directly on the stone, the student must realize that the final print will be the reverse of what is being drawn. With this in mind he may wish to make many of the features of his initial drawing in reverse in order to obtain the desired effects on the printed edition.

Only the following should be used to record the image: lithographic crayons, pencils, pens, tusche, or pigments that will interact with limestone, forming an isoluble lime soap on the surface, which in turn will receive the printing ink and repel water. Some types of felt pens contain enough grease substance to be very effective. Perhaps you may

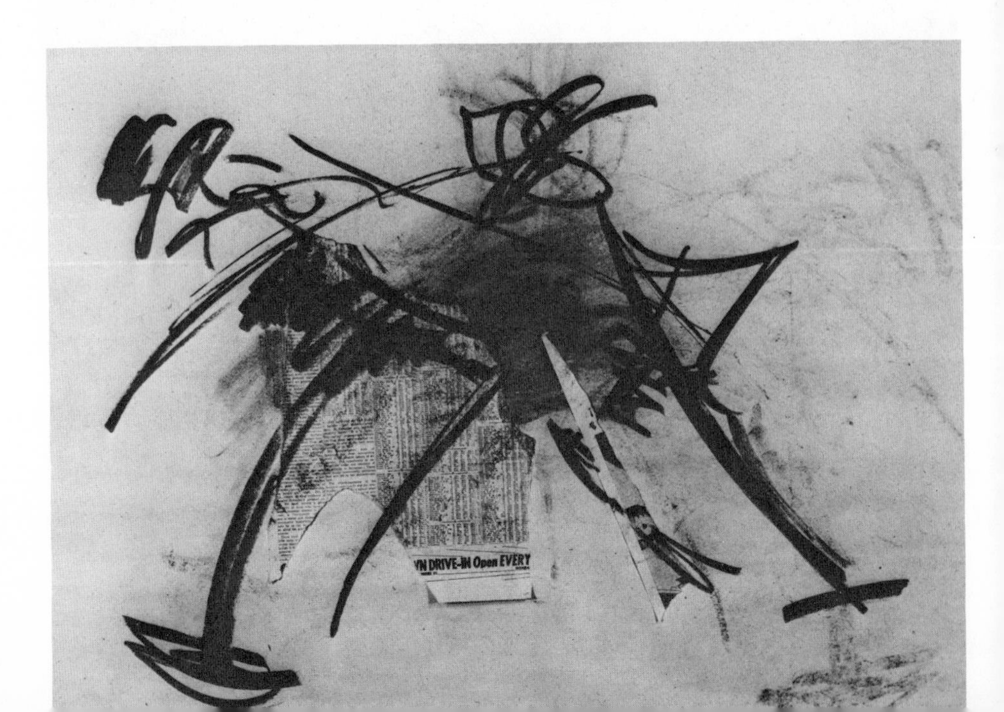

The gesture drawing created by using the broad side of a lithographic crayon depicts the feeling and mood of the subject. The high school student who drew these soldiers attempted to identify himself with the attitude of his models in action. Gesture drawings induce and persuade the individual engaged to participate kinesthetically.

discover others. It is most advisable for those who are beginners to use an experimental approach in drawing directly on the stone. They should attempt to achieve a variety of light and dark values by beginning with a light tone and gradually building up to darker tones and by gently going over and over the light areas until the desired tones are achieved. A variety of line quality can be achieved by using soft, medium soft, and hard pencils and gradually bearing down and letting up on the pencils while drawing. Attempts to obtain textured effects may be made by using tusche and asphaltum; by rubbing the ink into the stone with the tips of the fingers; by scraping and scratching into the greased areas with a sharp instrument; by burning the surface with diluted nitric acid; and by combining tusche, crayon, and asphaltum. The beginner, again, should be forewarned not to touch the printing surface with his hands; oil from the hands will react much like the lithographic pencils, receiving the printer's ink, and resulting in a smudged print.

The method of drawing directly on the stone is, perhaps, the best approach to lithography, but for the beginner there is still another effective approach. Instead of drawing directly on the stone, the student creates his image with the lithographic media on paper and transfers it to the stone. The transfer is done by either moistening the back of the drawing or heating the drawing and pressing the image against the stone. The transfer technique does not produce the rich grays and blacks of the direct approach, but neither does it reverse the design, which is in itself a great advantage for the inexperienced printmaker. The transferred drawing may be gone over with lithographic crayon or pencil if darker tones are desired.

"Pheasant" by Barry Cohen, Syracuse University. Lithographic prints are no better than the drawings conceived by the artist. Many hours went into this fine nature drawing before it was rendered into a lithographic print.

Etching the stone

When the printmaker considers his drawing tentatively complete, he may etch the stone. The term ''etch'' in this case is fallacious since the ''etching'' does not really effect any change in the level of the surface of the stone. The change which takes place is one of a chemical nature. It desensitizes those areas of the surface of the stone that have not been drawn upon with lithographic media, and fixes (prevents from spreading) those areas represented by the drawing.

Etch solution is prepared by dissolving gum arabic crystals in water, forming a sticky consistency resembling rubber cement. Strain about a pint through cheesecloth or nylon into a clean jar and add one-fourth to one ounce of nitric acid and stir well. The exact amount of nitric acid is usually dependent upon the temperature, humidity, and age of the nitric acid, as well as the quality of the grease on the stone. The heavier the grease and the warmer the day, the stronger the etch; the lighter the grease and the cooler the day, the weaker the etch. Metal plates, of course, require a different etch solution. In the use of zinc plates, the gum arabic is treated with chromic acid. Aluminum, on the other hand, requires a mixture of gum arabic and phosphoric acid.

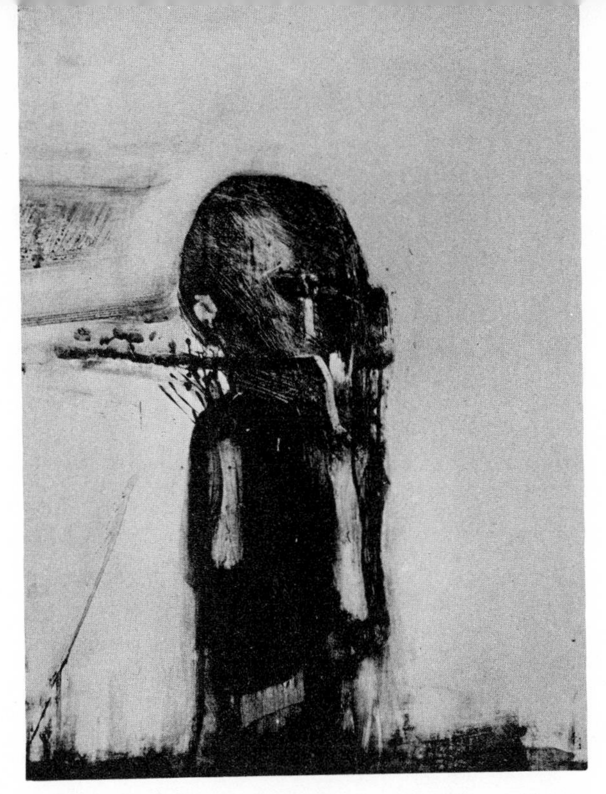

"The Flutist" by Nathan Oliveira, Urbana, Illinois.

The etch is poured on one area of the stone and with a sponge or rubber set brush is spread over the entire stone. With newsprint, the excess gum is blotted from the stone. The surface is then gently rubbed with the palm of the hand or with a pad of soft cloth and allowed to dry. It is highly recommended that etch be allowed to remain on the stone for at least twelve hours.

The next step is to remove the etch by washing the stone with water. The stone is then regummed and the crayon drawing removed with the aid of a pad of cheesecloth and turpentine. The image will remain. What is actually removed is the pencil carbon.

The stone is then dried thoroughly and washed again with clean water in order to remove any dissolved crayon particles. The stone is kept constantly wet in preparation for the inking. While the stone is still wet, an inked roller is passed over the entire stone surface several times or until the stone is sufficiently charged; the paper is printed in the same way as is litho sketchmaster paper.

Paper used in stone lithography must be dampened to allow it to become soft enough to make a good contact with the inked surface. It is therefore necessary to use a good grade of paper that will hold together, especially when using a press with a traveling bed requiring sliding pressure. Among the inexpensive but satisfactory papers, Arches or Rives, Basingwerk Parchment, Fiesta Cover Stock, and Navarre are recommended. If a roller-type printing press is used, any good grade of drawing paper is acceptable. In preparation, the paper is stacked between wet blotters or bogus paper, placed under slight pressure, and left for a few hours.

"Tahiti" by Carol Intemann, Syracuse University.

Plaster Lithography

The Tahiti landscape by Carol Intemann was made from a plaster plate. The plaster was made by casting plaster of Paris into a shoe box to about an inch in thickness. When the plaster was thoroughly dry, it was coated with shellac and covered with another layer of plaster one-eighth inch thick. The image was then drawn on the surface of the plaster plate, etched, inked, and printed in much the same manner as are the Bavarian limestones.

Color Lithography

Whereas we were once content to leave color lithography to the professional printmakers, we are today, with the advent of new techniques and innovations, taking up the challenge of color printing. Adding color to lithography is a simple and valuable asset. In addition to the use of separate plates, color may be obtained by superimposing a single lithographic plate on prepared backgrounds of colored ground paper or patterns of cut and torn colored construction paper pasted to what will ultimately be the ground paper. The excitement of color, along with the almost limitless possibilities of its incorporation, makes it the element which rounds out an already versatile medium.

Lithography with Metal Plates

Recently, printmakers have brought into use a grained metal plate, usually aluminum or zinc, which is much lighter, less expensive, and more flexible, and which can be adjusted to a rotary printing press. Most of the commercial firms today use metal lithographic plates with the image photographically reproduced upon them. The photographic principle is based upon the use of a plate coated with a special solution that hardens when exposed to light.

Photolithography is a process of great versatility and speed and has made it possible for almost anyone today to afford very presentable reproductions of great art works not obtainable by other means. Although it has numerous advantages for the commercial fields, it lacks challenge for the experimentally minded printmaker.

"Nocturnal Inscape" by George Lockwood, Boston, Massachusetts.

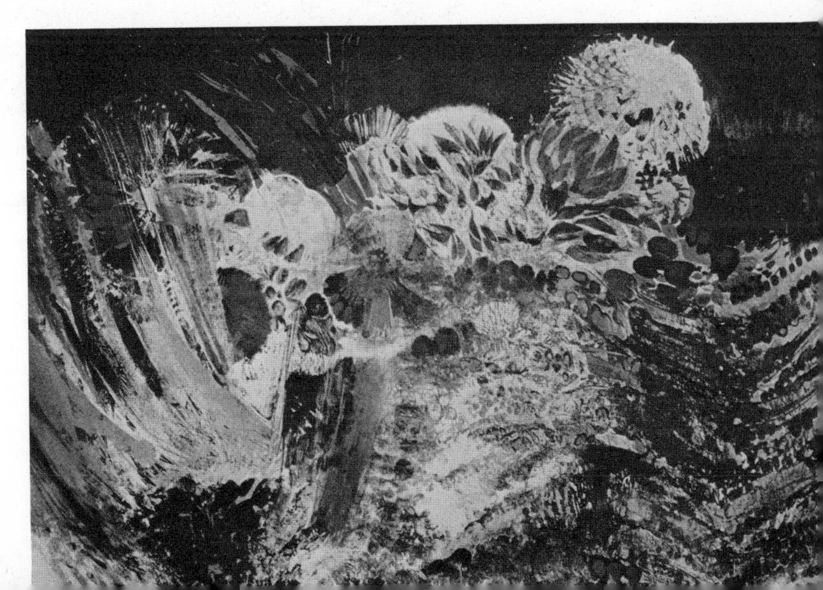

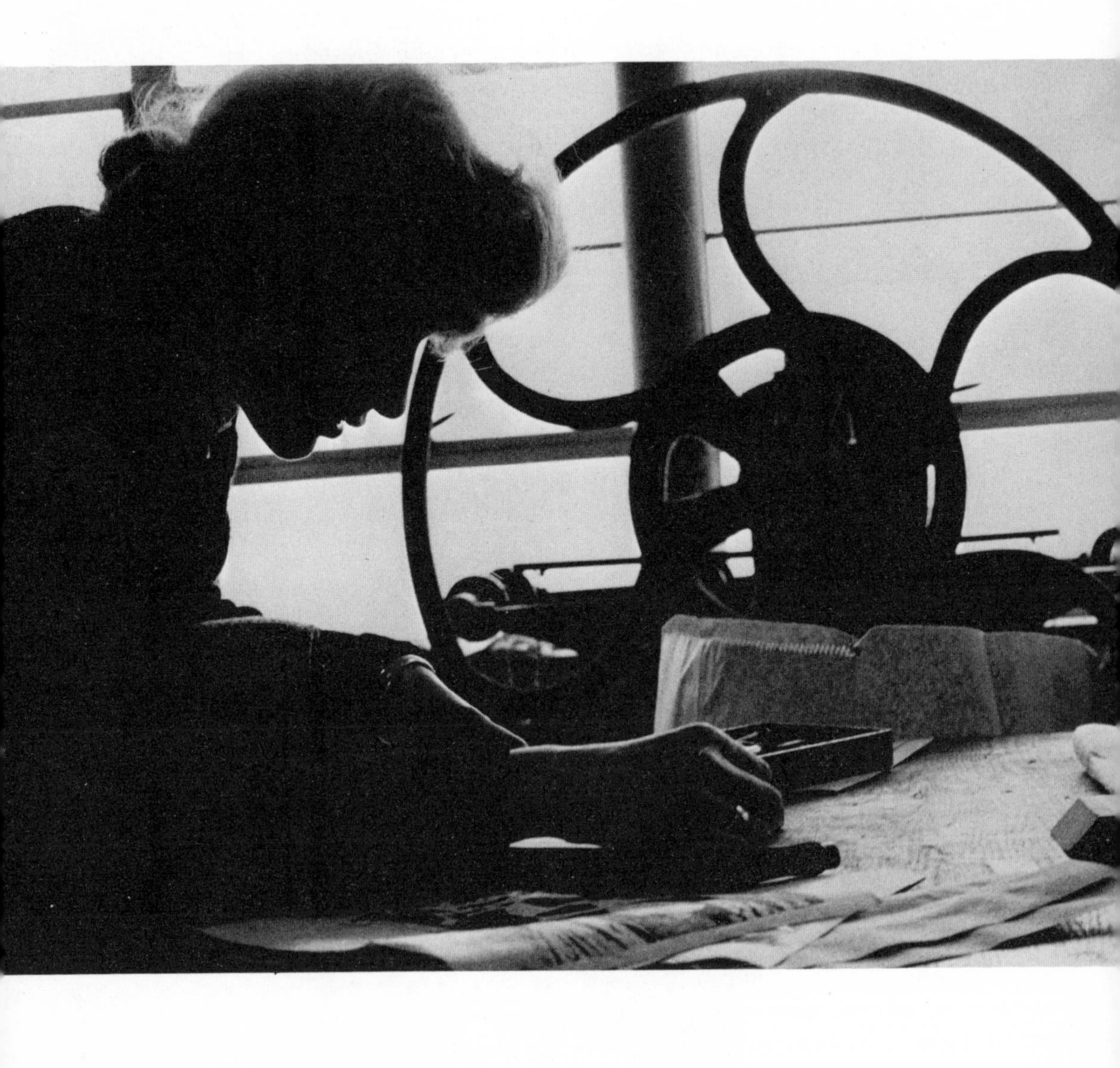

5

The Intaglio Printing Process

The technique of printing in intaglio is perhaps the most complex of all the printing processes. It requires strong concentration, considerable technical knowledge, and highly skilled methods that can be mastered only through arduous and diligent practice. It is, therefore, the most inappropriate printing process for use in the public schools. Perhaps only the experienced high school students who have a strong desire to acquire skills and proficiency should be encouraged to work in this technique. But since there are aesthetic values to be derived from the experiences that intaglio printing has to offer, we are obligated to attempt to modify the process so that we may provide the opportunity of such experiences to students at all levels.

The principles of intaglio printing are just the opposite of printing in relief. Instead of depositing the ink on the raised surface of the plate, the ink is forced into the incised lines and lower recesses of the plate and the surface is wiped clean. Dampened paper is then forced with considerable pressure against the plate and into the incisions in order to pick up the ink from the indentations which impart the image. Although the image is imparted from the recessed areas, as well as line, the printmaker is more likely to conceive of his image in terms of line rather than mass notations. In fact, when we look at an intaglio print, we usually gain some of the intimacy that exists between an artist and his pen-and-ink drawings.

There are a number of preliminary exercises which may be used before any introduction of the actual intaglio printing process. Since a print is no better than the idea it incorporates, consideration should be given, first and foremost, to the aesthetic principles of great art. Most prints have a predominantly linear quality as well as a less tangible sense of a certain mood or feeling, which reflects the artist's involvement with the subject. It is, therefore, advisable that line (contour and gesture) drawings be introduced as two salient exercises in developing these two qualities. The preliminary exercises will undoubtedly help the beginner dedicate his energies to the act of meaningful self-expression. To help the student come to some understanding and appreciation of the technical aspects of the eventual experience of genuine intaglio printing, simulated etching processes are also introduced here as preliminary technical exercises.

Gesture drawing with brush and tempera paint by a high school student.

Contour drawing with brush and India ink by a college student.

Contour Drawing

This method of drawing is not to be confused with the outline method of drawing in which children are permitted to draw the head, body, legs, and arms of a figure separately, that is, step by step. Nor is it to be construed as a silhouette drawing. Contour drawing is a two-dimensional interpretation of a three-dimensional object or scene. It attempts to represent perspective, foreshortening, and space relations by means of variations in pressure applied to the pencil, crayon, or brush. It is a simple and natural mode of outline drawing in which the outer edge of the object being depicted is set down in a continuous line as one sees it. The student is instructed to keep his eyes fixed at all times on the object being drawn. The pencil or crayon is placed on the paper in a position corresponding to a point on the object upon which the eyes are fixed. As the eyes follow the contours of the object, the pencil is moved slowly along the paper, in and around the entire object and returning to the original starting point. The student is instructed to avoid evaluating the results until after the drawing is completed. In the case of a complicated drawing it is permissible, from time to time, to lift the pencil from the paper in order to continue from another point. Although the eyes may be constantly fixed on the object, the student is actually drawing with the aid of his tactile sense. He should be encouraged to be fearless, courageous, and willing to accept his preliminary attempts. It should be explained to the student that these are not intended to be finished drawings but merely practice sessions for exercising his observation and line perception.

Gesture Drawing

The term "gesture" is used to describe a method of drawing which depicts the action, feeling, or mood of the subject. It is more concerned with the emotional qualities than with photographic accuracy. Gesture

"Lullaby" by Francis de Erderly, University of Southern California. *Courtesy of the artist.*

Drawing is a graphic language which provides opportunity for children and youth to express themselves. The product represents an autobiography of the student's vision, impressions, and interpretations of life as he lives it. Seldom does one find an artist with Francis de Erderly's skill and mastery in drawing.

drawings are done rapidly with a continuous movement of the arm and hand, hardly lifting the pencil off the paper. The pencil is pushed freely in imitation of the model.

This creative method of drawing usually provides encouragement to the student to interpret the attitude of the subject with his whole being. The student does not feel himself to be a discrete, separate entity, distinct from the subject that he is perceiving, but instead feels at one with what he perceives. The subject becomes an extension of the artist; it is not analyzed or observed objectively, nor is the drawing governed by logical coherence or art rules.

The subject being interpreted may be either an animate or inanimate object, present to the eye or conjured up from the imagination. Whatever the source, the student is encouraged to react to the subject kinesthetically. The teacher encourages the student to approach the subject without concern for his powers of analysis or observation. She

Gesture (action) drawing made with India ink and a plastic quill by a college student.

encourages him to merge his attitude with that of the model by identifying himself with it. If the model is a cat, for example, the student may pretend that he is the cat: in his mind, he may run along the floor, gracefully leap into a chair, and curl up for a short nap. The teacher may go so far as to encourage the student to act out the gestures with his hands, head, and body in dramatic gesture.

If the subject to be represented is a tree such as a poplar or an old oak, the young artist may attempt to capture the manner of its growth. He is encouraged to depict the tallness and straightness of the poplar or the rugged character of the oak. The character of the more inanimate models is often suggested by their inherent distinctions. For example, a steam roller is big, bold, heavy, and massive; a bicycle is narrow, light, and fleet; while a rock is rough, hard, and heavy. The gesture drawings of these objects should, therefore, attempt to capture and represent such feelings as weight, speed, delicacy, and solidity. Gesture drawings are not intended to look like the model. They are, instead, directed toward an expressive arrangement of form, line, and color for the purpose of indicating character. Gesture drawings usually look sketchy and aimless to anyone who cannot read them, but the benefits derived from such activity are beyond doubt. Gesture drawing induces and persuades the student to participate in the light of his own aesthetic experiences.

One of the best methods of preparing the students for intaglio printing is to have them begin with simulated intaglio techniques. Crayon etching and scratchboard, which have some relation to intaglio, are not literally printing processes; they are nevertheless two of the best methods of helping the students gain experience with the conception of line technique without having to spend too much time on the mechanical requirements of the actual printing process. They permit the students to experiment with gradation of line, as well as with line movement, and to adapt to the discipline and creative work habits of intaglio printing.

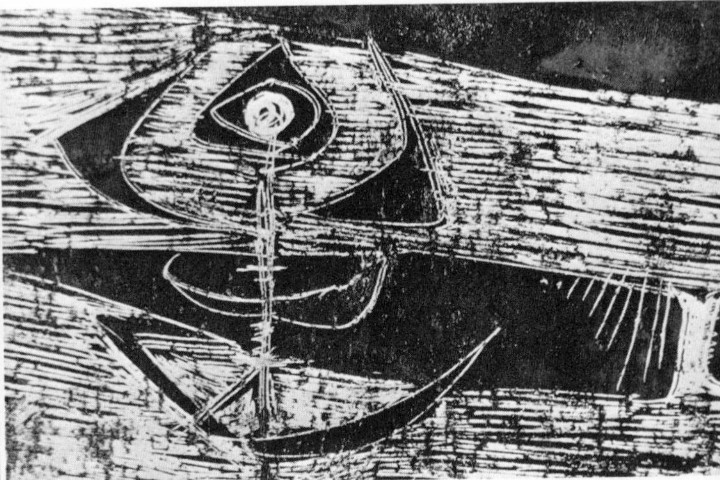

Crayon Etching

This technique is quite simple. White paper, preferably a glossy cardboard, is covered with a heavy coat of black wax crayon. Lines and mass areas are then scratched into the surface, revealing the white ground. The crayon etching paper may also be prepared by coating the surface first with a layer of white crayon and then with a heavy coat of black crayon, or by applying a coat of black India ink. Since the wax crayon has a tendency to resist the ink, it may be necessary to apply several coats. One may experiment with various types of paints, and combinations of paints, inks, and papers.

Scratchboard

The scratchboard technique is used quite frequently in the commercial art field, but may be considered an effective preliminary to etching. It permits sharp, precise lines and fine detail and is, therefore, a more appropriate medium for the junior and senior high school student. Although scratchboard is a fairly expensive, commercially prepared illustration board, students need not be deprived of this technique. The ingenious teacher can have the students prepare a reliable substitute by simply coating a glossy, hard-surface cardboard with India ink. After the surface has been coated and is thoroughly dry, the image is scratched into the surface with a sharp instrument, thereby removing the top layer of ink. The finished product may result in white line–dark background or black line–light background imagery.

After the student has had some experience with the preliminary exercises, he may begin to work in the literal printing processes. The dry-point and etching processes, because of their simplicity in terms of both the plates and the drawing instruments, are the best suited to introduce the public school student to intaglio printing. The more intricate processes of aquatint and mezzotint may be especially interesting to the experienced adolescent who has a strong desire to experiment and to test his advanced abilities. The complexities of aquatint and mezzotint make them less suitable for use in the lower grades. They can, however, be mastered by the high school student under the guidance of a competent teacher. These four techniques, which will be discussed in this chapter, are for those who are appropriately equipped and who seek a new and more exciting printing process.

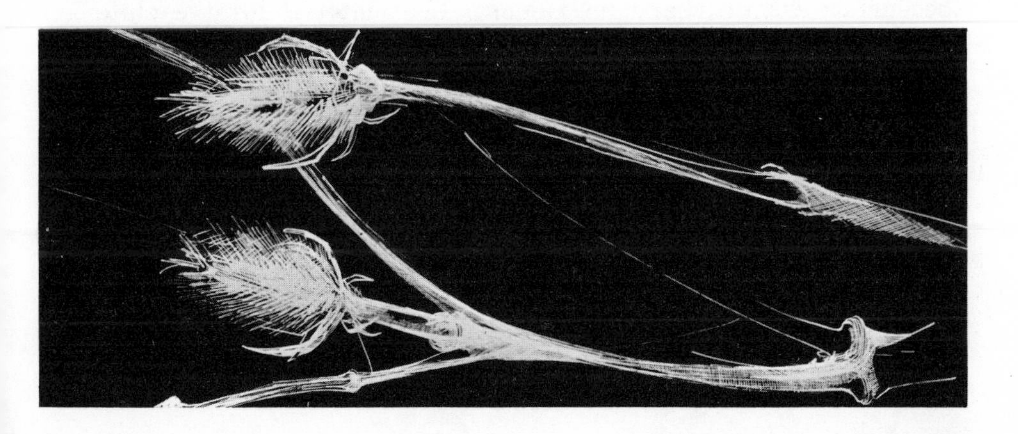

"Swan," a scratchboard drawing by Steve Gross, a college student.

Dry Point

Since dry point is one of the simplest of the intaglio processes and requires the least amount of equipment, it can be considered the logical introduction to intaglio printing. It is a practical process that can be carried out by most children in the upper grades with little or no technical difficulty. In dry point, the plate is created by scratching the surface with a sharp instrument. The material for the plate has been traditionally metal, such as copper, zinc, or brass; but celluloid, plastic, and old x-ray plates have been introduced for public school use. In fact, any scratchable, nonabsorbent material that will retain its shape may be used.

To begin with, the students should be encouraged to make several rough sketches from which they may select a good one to be carried out in the actual dry-point technique. Although the technique may seem to be very simple, it can be quite demanding. It is, therefore, recommended that the sketches be made relatively small so that they may be transferred to plates that are approximately four by six inches in size. The

"The Village," a dry point by Aviva Goldblatt, a college student, was made by scratching into a sheet of plastic. Waterbase printer's ink, soft paper, and a wringer-type press were used to reproduce the image.

student may be permitted to undertake a more demanding project only after he has experienced the process. Once the best sketch is selected, the celluloid or plastic plate is placed over it and the general idea of the rough sketch is scratched into the plate's surface. For this purpose, a dry-point needle or any sharp, needle-like instrument that is capable of scratching the plate may be used. The dry-point needle is most effective when held in the same manner as a pencil, pointing slightly in the direction toward which one is cutting. Any precise or faithful reproduction of the drawing or design should be avoided; it can only lead to a stiff, monotonous, lifeless composition. Just the general idea is copied; the actual detailed image should be cut spontaneously, and directly into the plate. In this way the resulting image will necessarily depict vitality and spontaneity.

In dry point there is actually no attempt to remove any of the plate. The material is merely relocated. The instrument used to scratch the plate turns up a furrow or "burr." When the plate is inked and wiped clean, the burr holds most of the ink, producing a soft, blurred, velvety, black-toned line in the print. Both the pressure applied and the angle at which the dry-point needle is held help determine the character of the lines. The lines may vary from barely visible scratches to heavy, bold indentations. Mass notations and dark values may be obtained by crosshatched or parallel lines cut close together. By removing the burr with a burnisher, one may effect gray tones. As the scratching technique progresses, the incised lines may be darkened with ink in order to accent them for observation and to assist in further modification of the design. Modifications and revisions are also possible after the first proof is pulled. The plate is cleaned and, with the aid of the dry-point needle, additional incisions are made. Any undesirable incisions are removed by simply burnishing the burr, thereby lessening its effectiveness. An incision cannot be completely obliterated. Care should therefore be taken in the initial scratching activity.

When the plate is completed, a little printer's ink is squeezed onto it, spread evenly over the entire surface with a dabber, the fingers, or the end of tightly rolled paper towels, and forced into the incised lines. The plate is then wiped clean with tarlatan or a wad of unbleached muslin. Since it is not possible to wipe the plate entirely clean, ink left in and around the burr will produce the characteristics of the incised lines in the print. Various tonal values can be obtained by controlled wiping of the plate. The proper transfer of ink to paper requires a considerable amount of pressure. The most satisfactory results are obtained by using a washing machine wringer or a roller-type press. A

sheet of damp paper is placed over the image and then covered with several blotters or a felt pad. The plate, thus prepared, is carefully put through the press. The plate is cleaned and carefully re-inked before each printing. Since the dry-point technique relies on the burr—a rather fragile edge—an inexpensive press which applies less pressure is best used. It is quite possible to get acceptable prints by applying pressure with the spoon-rubbing method or by hand-pressing.

Each material used for making plates will have its own character. It would, therefore, be unfortunate if the students were not encouraged to find new materials and to explore their possibilities. In addition to celluloid and plastic, soft metal plates may be used to make dry-point prints. Unfortunately, the burr is gradually broken down by the repeated wiping and the pressure of the press. Only a small edition is possible by this method of intaglio printing.

Engraving

In making a dry point or an etching, the technique is not unlike that of using a pencil or brush; but in doing an engraving, a completely different process is involved. The instrument, usually a burin or graver, is pushed, like a linoleum cutter, rather than pulled across the surface of the plate. As with the dry point, incisions are made directly into the plate. The lowered areas which result are, however, somewhat different in character from the lines of the dry point. Since, in engraving, the artist actually removes part of the plate rather than merely relocating it, the resulting lines will be more distinct and precise.

Engraving may at first seem relatively simple, but it is actually very difficult, requiring great craftsmanship and determination. The technical virtuosity and great precision which are possible in engraving have made it the logical method for printing money, stamps, and important documents. The United States Bureau of Engraving has carried engraving to such levels of precision that plates for currency are extremely difficult to reproduce.

The elementary school and, possibly, the high school student will not approach the level of precision possible in this medium. The execution of curved and curling lines, and of other changes in direction, requires great skill in turning and twisting the plate while engraving. The direct involvement and complexity of engraving do, however, make it an interesting and valuable experience for public school students. They are forced to think before taking positive action. This necessity of complete forethought is in keeping with the educational goal of developing critical awareness.

Traditionally, engraving has been done on plates of copper, zinc, and brass; but, as with dry point, the plate may be of any material that can be cut away with a sharp instrument. A variation of this technique that may be used in the public schools is one in which paper and metal foils are indented, inked, and printed. Since no material is actually removed, this technique is not truly engraving; but it is similar enough to be considered a very good introductory process for the beginner.

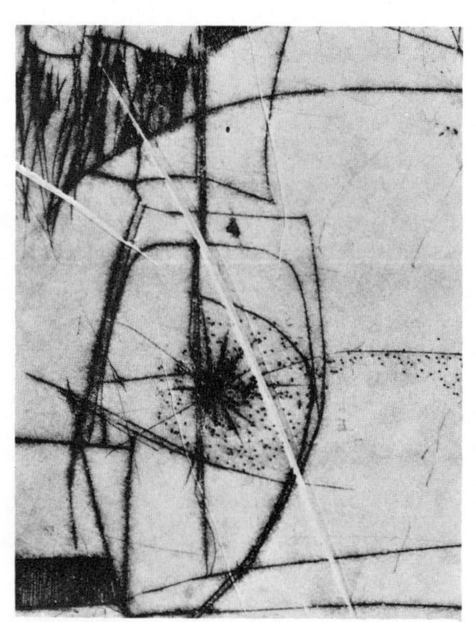

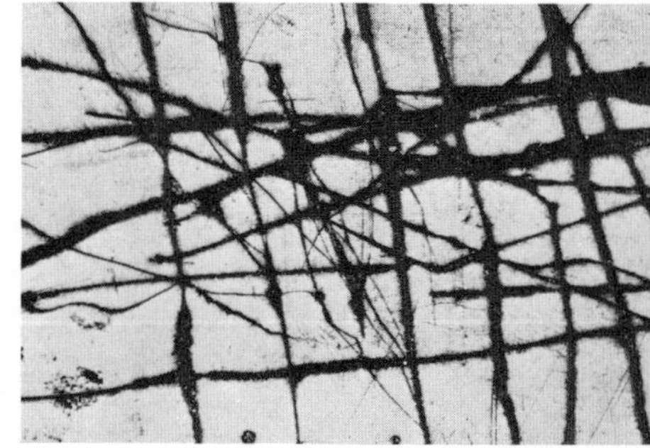

Simple etchings by two junior high school boys who used nails as tools and sheets of metal taken from galvanized cans.

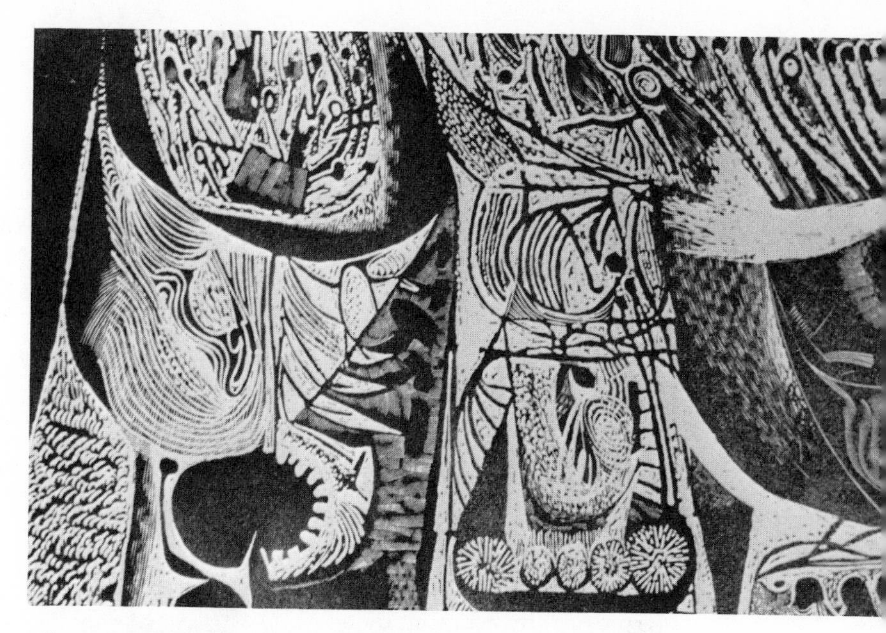

"The Insects Go Up: Yucatan" (detail) by Arthur Deshaies, Peterborough, New Hampshire. *Courtesy of the artist.*

The design or drawing on engraving plates may be prepared with a marking pencil or wax crayon. If the plate has a dull finish, soft lead pencils can be used. Caution must be taken, however, not to smudge the drawing. Teachers and students should experiment with different materials and tools.

Etching

The most involved and versatile of the intaglio processes is etching. Although best suited to the advanced high school students, it can be taught without extreme difficulty to small groups of eighth-, seventh-, and even sixth-graders, if they are handled with special care and proper guidance.

The principle of etching is to print from the lower portion of a metal plate that has been created by means of acid. The metal plates generally used are copper, zinc, or aluminum alloy. Other materials that may be used are lucite and masonite. Sixteen - or eighteen-gauge copper, however, is undoubtedly the best for those who desire to do fine, delicate work; but zinc and aluminum are much more economical

"The Knight, Death, and the Devil" (engraving) by Albrecht Dürer. *Courtesy of The Brooklyn Museum.*

and just as effective. Moreover, since zinc reacts more quickly to the acid bath, it is perhaps the most practical for public school use. Precut metal plates may be purchased from art supply stores. If additional cutting is necessary, it should be done by a precision machine, to prevent the smooth surface from becoming impaired. The edges of the metal plate should be carefully beveled and the corners rounded to prevent them from cutting into the paper or blanket during the printing. The beveling is best done with a flat, fine-toothed file.

The basic procedure for preparing the plate for the art work is to cover it with an acid-resisting ground that will protect the plate, allowing the etching action to take place only where the drawing has been scratched through the ground. Among several materials which may be used as a ground are asphaltum, shellac, stop-out varnish, and commercially prepared compositions of wax, resin, and pitch. These are considered hard grounds, but may easily be converted into soft grounds by adding an equal amount of tallow or vaseline and mixing thoroughly.* The plate is grounded by first being heated on a hotplate and then being evenly coated with the ground preparation. A dabber,

* For soft-ground etching see page 129.

roller, or soft brush is used to apply the ground. Since the ground is approximately the same color as the plate, most printmakers prefer to smoke the ground so that the plate can be seen as the lines are incised, facilitating the drawing process. The plate is held horizontally, with the ground-side down, over a burning candle or bunsen burner, so that the carbon is deposited on the ground. Care is taken not to touch the flame to the ground or to hold the plate in one spot too long, which will cause the ground to become overheated and melt.

The artist can now scratch his creative idea into the ground, preparing it for the step that follows—etching the plate. The image is scratched into the coated plate with the aid of a blunt-pointed, needle-like instrument. An ordinary darning needle placed in a pen holder, or a short piece of doweling rod, works most effectively. Roulettes, échoppes, and sandpaper may also be used to achieve special textured effects. Just enough pressure is applied to these instruments to cause them to remove the ground, exposing the plate to the acid.

Although many teachers prefer to translate from a drawing on paper, it is best to compose directly on the ground. The students should be encouraged to be daring and to experiment with and explore the various possibilities in creating a design so that the print does not become merely a mechanical reproduction of a drawing.

In the final preparation for the actual etching, the edges and back of the plate are coated with an acid-resisting material and placed in a tray of acetic acid. This will remove any grease from the areas to be etched, thus allowing the stronger acid to bite equally over the entire plate.

"Silent Rider" (intaglio) by John Vargo, Syracuse University. *Courtesy of the artist.*

The plate is then submerged in a bath of nitric or iron perchloride acid and etched. Six parts of water are used to each part of nitric acid. If iron perchloride is used, an equivalent amount of water is added. Avoid any direct contact with the acid. Should the skin touch the acid, wash immediately with water. If the skin appears to be burning, apply bicarbonate of soda. The use of rubber gloves is recommended in lowering the plate into and retrieving it from the acid bath.

The depth and width of the resulting depressions are dependent upon the strength and type of acid used, the temperature of the room, and the length of time the plate remains in the acid. Nitric acid tends to widen as well as to deepen the lines; iron perchloride, which is similar to the Dutch mordant used by Rembrandt, etches deeply but will not widen the lines.

There are several ways of etching with acid; some ways produce a variety of effects. In addition to submerging the entire plate in a tray of acid, one may make a tray out of the plate itself by building a wall of wax around the areas to be etched. Another method is to apply drops of acid, continuously and in small amounts, on the desired areas of the plate. Since it weakens as it etches, acid must be added throughout the process. Still another method would be that of inscribing the lines which will be etched the deepest, submerging the plate for a given time, retrieving the plate and scratching those lines which are to be a little more shallow, and returning the plate to the acid bath. The process is continued for each level of depth desired. The reverse of this procedure would be first to scratch the lines that are intended to be the faintest and, after etching these, to remove the plate, wash and dry it, and apply stop-out to prevent further etching. Each successive

"Feigele" (detail of an intaglio) by Alfred Blaustein, New York City. *Courtesy of the artist.*

series of lines is etched deeper by being allowed to etch longer. Gas bubbles may appear along the lines being etched. When this happens they should be removed with a feather or a pipe cleaner, or by tilting the tray, exposing the affected part of the plate to the air. The depth of depressions can be determined by feeling them with the point of an etching needle.

When the plate has been completely etched, the ground is removed with the appropriate solvent. The plate is then covered with printer's ink, wiped clean, and printed in much the same manner as described in the dry-point method.

Etching is the only intaglio process in which smooth gray values, as well as black lines, may be produced. Its richness of texture and tonalities can be achieved in two principal ways. The first is the hard-ground process previously described. The lines from hard grounding are usually precise and sharp. The second type is called soft-ground etching. Soft ground differs from hard ground in that it is more susceptible to impressions, because of the added softness of the ground. A sheet of fine paper is placed over the grounded plate and drawn upon with a pencil. Wherever the pencil presses against the soft ground, it forces the paper to adhere to the plate. When the paper is pulled away, it lifts the ground from the plate, exposing the metal. The plate is then submerged in the acid bath and etched like the hard-grounded plate. Soft-ground prints have the same quality as a pencil drawing or lithograph. In addition to paper, a piece of cloth, burlap, screen, or lace may be used to obtain variations in texture. The somewhat accidental quality of some of the surfaces available may encourage freedom and explorations not possible in other intaglio methods.

"Boats, Sails, and Umbrellas" (etching) by Renzo Vespegnani. *In The Brooklyn Museum Collection.*

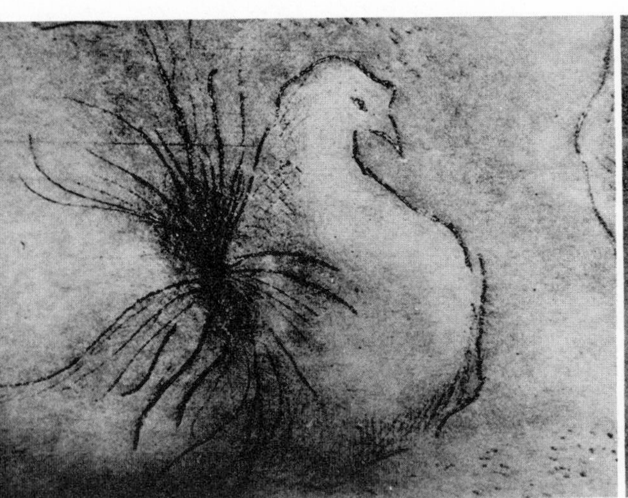

"Doves" (etching) by Michelle Ryan, a college student, was made from a precoated aluminum plate. The specially prepared plate was engraved, placed in an etch bath made of etching powder mixed with water, and printed in the simple manner prescribed in the text.

The etching above was done on a precoated aluminum etching plate. These plates are manufactured with a thin, acid-resistant coating which eliminates the necessity of tediously grounding the plate. The image is scratched directly into the plate with a sharp instrument.

The process is further simplified by the use of a solution of water and etching powder.* One teaspoonful of etching powder to one cup of water is recommended. Unlike regular etch, this solution is nonpoisonous and harmless to the hands.

As the solution etches the plate, a black sediment will appear in the lines. It is imperative that this sediment be removed repeatedly during the etching, to facilitate the process. One may use a feather or a pipe cleaner to remove the sediment, or one may remove the plate from the etch bath, wash the sediment off, and return the plate to the bath. If the sediment stops forming, the etch solution has become weak and should be replenished with etching powder.

* The precoated aluminum plate, as well as the etching powder, may be obtained from the Rembrandt Graphic Arts Company, Incorporated, of Stockton, New Jersey.

"Icarus Ante Volantum" (polymar on aluminum) by Dean Meeker, University of Wisconsin. *Courtesy of the artist.*

Mezzotint

The mezzotint technique is, as the term implies (mezzo = middle, tint = shade), a process of creating a variety of middle-gray tones. Instead of the linear quality found in the other two more mechanical processes of intaglio printing (dry point and etching), one finds in mezzotint the concept of form and chiaroscuro.

The basic principle in preparing a mezzotint plate to achieve this concept of form is to rough up the surface of the plate until it is capable of printing a rich, dark tone, and, after the design has been transposed, to scrape and burnish areas of the surface to produce lighter and contrasting values. The graining of the plate is done with a rocker, which is a special curved tool, with many sharp cutting edges, designed to dig into the metal as it is rocked back and forth and in different directions across the plate, turning up burrs of metal.

Where there is very little special equipment available, indentations may be produced by placing a sheet of sandpaper over the top of a soft copper or zinc plate and passing it through a press, applying a sufficient amount of pressure to grain the plate. This procedure will have to be repeated at least a dozen times, each time with an unused piece of sandpaper. This will assure a proper graining. The degree of sandpaper grit will determine the size and frequency of the dents and thus govern the resulting gray tones.

The grain or burr is then cut or scraped away to produce subtle gradations and transitions of values. The more pressure that is applied, the lighter the value. If a white area is desired, the grain is removed completely and the surface is thoroughly burnished. The roulette and burin may be used to rework or reburr certain areas and to add to line accents and desired detail. Since the infinite number of burrs acts as a blotter, absorbing a great deal of the oil from the ink, it is especially wise to use a printer's ink that is a little oilier than the ink used for other intaglio processes.

"Catherine, Lady Bampfylde" (mezzotint) by Thomas Watson after Sir Joshua Reynolds. *Courtesy of the National Gallery, Washington, D.C. (Rosenwald Collection).*

Aquatint

The aquatint is another of the intaglio techniques of producing tonal values. However, whereas the mezzotint technique emphasizes the change of values in an object from light to dark, aquatint is a process of producing broad areas of flat tones; and although aquatint is capable of providing a limitless variation of tonal values, from white through the grays to strong blacks, it is not conducive to the concept of modeling. In fact, aquatint is usually thought of as an independent process done solely in tonal values; nevertheless it does lend itself effectively to an interplay of mass and line expression. Care must be taken, however, when using variation of values and line etching not to lose the simplicity and flat character of the aquatint. Aquatint is a process of etching through a resin ground especially prepared on a copper or zinc plate. The plate is grounded by dusting its surface evenly with powdered resin that has been placed in a piece of cheesecloth, nylon stocking, or China silk and tied into a small bag. The resin bag is held about six inches above the plate and tapped gently with a pencil or the index finger so that the resin sifts through to the surface of the plate. The fineness or coarseness of the resin dust laid on the plate's surface helps to determine the quality of the grain to be printed. The mesh of the material used in making the resin bag determines, in part, the quality of the resin dust deposited, and thus also helps to affect the grain of the print. A number of dusting bags may be used in attempting to obtain and control the variation of resin quality. Care should be taken to keep the dusting bag in constant motion while sifting, especially if one desires to obtain a uniformity in the tonal quality of the resulting surface. Caution should also be taken to do the dusting in an area where there is no breeze or draft that will cause an uneven distribution of dust to settle over the plate.

Another way of grounding the plate is to dissolve particles of resin in denatured alcohol and to coat the plate with the solution. The proportions are determined by the effect one desires to obtain. The alcohol eventually evaporates, leaving the resin affixed in a crackled surface to the plate.

After the plate is grounded, it is carefully placed on a hot plate and heated sufficiently to cause the resin particles to melt and adhere to the plate. When the resin particles appear wet and colorless, like beads of sweat, and the plate begins to smoke a little, the plate is removed and allowed to cool. Each droplet of resin becomes an acid-resistant dot surrounded by exposed portions of the plate that are vulnerable to the acid, which pits the area, creating crevices that will hold the ink in the printing of the plate. The tones of aquatint are literally produced by the ink in the irregular patterns etched around these tiny resin droplets. During this process care should be taken not to underheat or overheat the plate. When underheated, the light coating of resin will produce a rough grain on the plate; when overheated, the resin droplets run together and tend to coagulate and completely cover the plate's surface, defeating the principle of an aquatint. Any area which is not to be aquatinted, such as those which are to print white, as well as the edge and back of the plate are stopped-out with an acid-resisting material, preferably asphaltum.

The plate is then immersed in iron perchloride, Dutch mordant, or a solution of nitric acid. Since much more of the plate is exposed to the acid bath in the aquatint process than in the other processes, a much milder solution of nitric acid is recommended (nine parts of water to one part of nitric acid).

The lightest tone areas are etched first for a few minutes—the time depends upon the strength of the acid bath—and stopped-out. The plate is then removed from the bath, washed, and dried. The lightest intermediate tone area is then stopped-out with asphaltum and allowed to dry. The plate is returned to the bath for another period of etching.

"The Letter" (colorprint with dry point and aquatint) by Mary Cassatt. *Courtesy of the National Gallery of Art, Washington, D.C. (Rosenwald Collection).*

It is removed, washed, dried, and stopped-out before each etching process. The areas to be printed the darkest are etched the deepest. A lithographic crayon may be used along the edge of the stop-out solution to prevent the etching of an otherwise hard edge between the printing areas.

When the plate is completely etched, it is rinsed in water and cleaned with benzol or an appropriate stop-out solvent. The plate is now ready to be inked, wiped, and printed in the same manner as previously described.

There are a number of other methods of preparing the ground of an aquatint plate with which one may experiment. One of the most appropriate for the high school student would be to apply a sheet of sandpaper face down on the surface of a grounded plate, in much the same manner as in preparing for a mezzotint, and run it through the press using slightly less pressure than is used in the actual printing. The correct amount of pressure is most important. Another simple but effective method would be to apply an offset ground by pressing a textured material coated with hard ground to the surface of a heated plate, depositing the textural quality of the material onto the plate. For the more adventurous, a number of other slightly more complex methods of grounding an aquatint plate may be found in the books listed in the bibliography.

"Los Caprichos" (etching and aquatint) by Francisco Goya. *Courtesy of the National Gallery of Art, Washington, D.C. (Rosenwald Collection).*

Glossary

Acetic acid A mild acid used by printmakers for cleaning their metal plates.

Agitation A process used in developing film and printing the negative. It involves a gentle rocking of the tray containing the developer for a few seconds during the developing period.

Air painting A method of printing in which pigment is blown through a reed or tube, over a mask stencil.

Aperture An opening, such as found in a camera, which admits light.

Aquatint A method of etching which uses a porous, resin ground to obtain tonal areas from the metal plate.

Asphaltum A composition of asphalt rock and bitumen used to cover or stop-out acid when etching a plate.

Baren An instrument used to burnish the back of paper when printing from an inked relief block.

Bath An acid-proof container in which metal plates are etched; also, an acid solution used for etching purposes.

Bench hook A device used to hold a relief block while cutting. It may be referred to also as a jig.

Bevel A process of rounding the edges of a stone or metal plate. The rounded, smooth edge of a stone or plate is referred to as a beveled edge.

Bite The etching action of acid on metal plates.

Blanket A felt pad used on metal plates which are being run through an etching press.

Bleeding Oil or grease seepage around a printed line or form.

Blueprint A photographic print, white on a blue ground.

Box camera A simple, light-tight box with a single lens aperture and shutter speed regulator at one end and film at the other. The *Pinhole camera* is much like the box camera except that it has a fine, clean pinhole in place of a lens.

Brayer A rubber-, gelatin-, felt-, or leather-covered roller used in inking metal plates, linoleum, and wood blocks.

Bunsen burner A small gas and air burner which burns with intense heat.

Burin A pointed, steel tool used by engravers to cut into metal plates and the end-grain of wood blocks.

Burn Occurs when too much adhering fluid is used on nu film or pro film. The film "burns" or dissolves beyond the point of adherence.

Burnisher A highly polished, oval-shaped tool used to polish the incised lines or rough surfaces on a metal plate.

Burr A thin, rough edge made by a dry-point needle as it is drawn across a metal plate.

Camera obscura A darkened chamber having an aperture through which light from external objects enters to form an image on the surface opposite. A lense is usually used.

Carborundum An abrasive in solid or powder form which is used for graining.

Charged To load a brush or brayer with paint or ink.

Chase A box-like enclosure or case used to hold narrow lithographic stones during printing; used with roller-type press.

Chiaroscuro The gradation of color from shade to light.

Cliché verre A process of photographically printing a negative that has been made by coating the surface of a glass slab or piece of plastic or plexiglas with a pigment and scratching out the desired image. By painting in the desired image on the glass, a white impression on black background can be obtained.

Collage A work of art made by "pasting" a variety of textured papers, string, wood, and the like on a flat surface in an interesting pattern.

Collagraphic print (*See* Collagraphy.)

Collagraphy The process of making a relief print from a collage.

Composite print A print made up from a number of different stencils, plates, or blocks; especially multicolor prints.

Composition The quality of being put together in such a way as to produce a harmonious, aesthetic whole.

Contact print A print made with the negative in contact with the sensitive photographic paper or plate.

Cropping The framing of a desired portion of a photograph through removal of the undesirable in order to obtain an aesthetic composition.

Dabber A pad of cotton, usually covered with leather, used to ink a plate or to lay a ground.

Daguerreotype The earliest photographic process (1839). It used silver-coated metallic plates.

Darkroom A room, protected from light rays, for handling sensitive paper and plates.

Depth of field The area, in front of and behind the sharply focused subject, which appears acceptably in focus in the camera.

Desensitize A process of rendering a lithographic stone or paper plate insentitive to printer's ink by using an agent which has an antipathy to grease.

Developer A chemical agent used in developing photographs.

Diffusion The reflection of light by a rough, reflecting surface, or the transmission of light through a translucent material.

Dodging A method of controlling print density by shading various parts of the image during exposure to light.

Double exposure Two exposures, inadvertently or advertently producing an undesired or desired effect in a photograph.

Dry point A method of intaglio printing in which the metal or plastic plate has been scratched into with a steel point; also a print obtained from such a plate.

Dry-point needle (*See* Etching needle.)

Dust bag A bag made of silk or nylon and filled with resin dust for use in the aquatint process.

Dust box An airtight box used to collect resin dust and deposit it as a ground on metal plates for use in aquatinting.

Dusting The process of applying resin dust to the surface of a plate being prepared for aquatinting.

Dutch mordant A special acid solution prepared for use in fine etching.

Échoppe An oblique-faced etching needle used to obtain the swelled character of engraved lines.

Edition A special issue of prints taken at one time from a stone, block, metal plate, or screen.

Emulsion A suspension of sensitive silver salt in a viscous medium, used for coating film or plates.

End grain That flat surface of a block of wood which runs perpendicular to the grain.

Engraver's pad A leather-covered, sand-filled pad upon which the engraver supports his plate while engraving.

Engraving The process of cutting a design into metal, wood, or plastic by means of a sharp instrument, usually a burin or graver, for the express purpose of making an intaglio print; also, a print obtained from an engraved plate.

Enlarger An instrument used to enlarge an image of the negative by projecting it through a lens onto a photographic printing surface.

Etching The process of biting into a metal plate with corrosive acid to form a design to be printed on paper; also, a print obtained from an etched plate.

Etching needle An instrument with a steel point used to cut through the ground of a plate which is to be etched.

Exposure meter An instrument that measures light intensity and relates shutter speed, f-stop, and the film speed.

Extender A white, paste-like substance which is added to textile and silk screen paints to increase the volume and to add body.

Feathering A process of removing the corrosive material from an area being etched by acid, using a feather, pipe cleaner, or small brush.

Fixing solution (*See* Hypo.)

Flash bulb (*See* Flood lamp.)

Flood lamp An incandescent lamp burning under an overload of electricity, used to produce an intensity of light for photographic purposes; also referred to as a photo flood. The flash bulb serves the same purpose, but whereas the flood lamp is constant, the flash bulb is explosive and instantaneous.

Focus The act of giving proper sharpness to an image which is about to be photographed.

Foreshorten To represent a subject as diminished in such a way that it complies with the laws of perspective and thus appears to be of the proper size.

Foul bite The uncontrolled etching of a plate, caused by improper grounding.

Ghost An impression that is accidentally made by offset from discarded plates or waste paper.

Graining Preparing a smooth drawing surface of a lithographic stone by grinding with an abrasive.

Graver (*See* Burin.)

Ground An acid-resistant coating of wax, resin, or asphaltum, which is applied to a metal plate. The image is scratched through the ground, permitting the acid to etch the plate.

Hard ground A thin, acid-resistant layer of asphaltum, shellac, or varnish, which is put on a plate in preparing for an etching.

Hydrogen peroxide An oxidizing and bleaching agent used to obtain a deeper blue in making blueprints. Potassium alum may also be used.

Hypo Sodium hyposulfite, used as a fixing agent in photographic printing; also referred to as "fixing solution."

Impression A print made from an inked plate or block which has been subjected to pressure; also referred to as an "imprint."

Imprint (*See* Impression.)

India ink A black, permanent pigment made of lampblack or ivory black and used for drawing and painting.

Ink slab A large piece of glass, marble, or some other hard, nonabsorbent surface upon which ink may be prepared.

Intaglio An incised or engraved impression in a durable material, designed to yield a print when inked and subjected to pressure; also, a print obtained from such a plate.

Iron perchloride A chloride used on previously bitten metal plates.

Jig (*See* Bench hook.)

Latent image An invisible image produced by the effect of light on matter (usually silver halide), which can be rendered visible by the subsequent chemical process of photographic development.

Lens A transparent, optical glass which gathers rays of light from the scene and transmits them to the light-sensitive film or plate on which the image is recorded.

Linoleum block A piece of battleship linoleum into which has been cut an impression to be printed in relief; also a print obtained from such a block.

Linoleum cut (*See* Linoleum block.)

Linoleum print (*See* Linoleum block.)

Lithograph A planographic print made by the process of lithography.

Lithographic crayon A grease crayon or pencil used to draw upon a lithographic stone or litho sketchmaster paper in preparing a lithographic print.

Litho plate solution A specially prepared solution used to desensitize litho sketchmaster paper.

Lithographic print (*See* Lithograph.)

Lithographic press A press that works on a scraper principle and is used exclusively for lithographic printing.

Lithographic roller A roller used in lithographic printing. It has a solid wooden core wrapped in flannel and covered with leather.

Litho-sketch print A print made from sketchmaster paper. (*See* Sketchmaster paper.)

Lithographic stone A hard, porous limestone which has an affinity for both oil and water. These stones are usually imported from Bavaria.

Lithography A planographic printing process which depends upon the antipathy of grease or oil and water. Impressions are drawn with a grease crayon on stone or chemically prepared paper which is desensitized, inked, and printed.

Mask stencil A stencil in which the paint or ink is applied to the background around the outer margins of the (mask) image.

Mezzotint An intaglio process in which the plate's surface is roughened with a tool called a rocker to create a dark, textured surface, certain areas of which are lightened by burnishing and scraping; also a print obtained from such a plate.

Monoprint (*See* Monotype.)

Monotype A process of making a single print from a plate upon which an impression has been created with finger paint, oils, or inks; also a print obtained from such a process.

Mordant Any corroding agent used in printmaking to etch metal plates.

Negative A film or plate used in printing positive pictures.

Nitric acid A corrosive liquid, HNO_2, recommended for use in etching metal plates.

Offset A distinct transfer of an impression from one surface to another.

Oil stone A whetstone used with oil for sharpening burins, scrapers, and other such tools.

Photoelectric cell An instrument whose electrical properties are modified by the action of light, used to measure the intensity of light.

Photo flood lamp (*See* Flood lamp.)

Photograms A process of printing the silhouette image of objects by placing them on photographic paper, exposing it to light for a few seconds, and developing.

Photographic paper A specially prepared paper coated with a mixture of barium sulphate and gelatin to eliminate surface pores and to provide a smooth surface for a light-sensitive emulsion containing silver bromide.

Photography A process of printing images or designs on sensitized paper by the action of light.

Photolithography An offset process of lithography which involves photography as a means of producing the design on the plate.

Pinhole camera (*See* Box camera.)

Planography The art of printing from a flat surface which is neither raised nor incised.

Plastiline A nonhardening clay composed of tallow, pumice, powdered sulphur, earth clay, and varied plasticizers such as petroleum derivatives or linseed oil.

Plate A block, stone, stencil, or other material upon which an image has been carved, drawn, or etched for the express purpose of printing.

Plexiglas A fairly hard, transparent medium which resembles glass; comes in various colors as well as opaque, and can be cut with a saw, heated, and formed into different shapes.

Polaroid A precision camera which takes, develops, and prints its own photographs in a period of ten seconds.

Potassium alum (*See* Hydrogen peroxide.)

Proof A trial print obtained from a block, plate, or screen for the purpose of being studied and corrected.

Pull The act of peeling a print from a block, plate, or stone.

Redlights (*See* Safelights.)

Register To exact correspondence of separate blocks, plates, or screens in multicolor printing in order to assure proper alignment.

Relief printing A process of printing from a raised or projected surface; also a print obtained by such a process.

Resin An organic wax substance which melts when heated and is primarily used as a ground for aquatints.

Resin bag A bag made of silk or nylon, filled with resin dust and used to sprinkle resin as ground on metal plates.

Rocker An instrument in the shape of a rocker which contains many sharp points—used to roughen metal plates in preparation for printing mezzotints.

Roulette A wheeled or rotating, disk-like tool used to produce dots on engraving plates or to roughen a plate in altering a mezzotint.

Rubbings A reproductive technique of making impressions of incised and raised designs by pressing dampened rice paper over the block and rubbing it with a pencil, chalk, or pad coated with ink.

Safelights A red light used in a photographic darkroom to aid the photographer in seeing without exposing the sensitized paper.

Scraper A tool used to remove burrs from metal plates; also used to incise heavy lines.

Scratchboard A smooth-surfaced, lightweight cardboard which is designed to be coated with crayon or ink and scratched through for the desired impressions.

Serigraph (*See* Serigraphy.)

Serigraphy A process of stencil printing in which the pigment is forced through a silk screen. A print obtained by such a process is called a serigraph.

Shutter A mechanical device attached to a camera and used to permit the proper amount of light to expose the film or plate.

Silk screen (*See* Serigraphy.)

Silver bromide Microscopic crystals which are sensitive to light. They register their encounter with light by turning black during the developing of the negative.

Silver chloride A compound that is sensitive to light and used to produce light-sensitive paper.

Sketchmaster paper A specially prepared, sensitized paper which when drawn upon with a grease crayon and desensitized produces a lithographic print.

Soft ground A ground to which nonhardening agents such as vaseline or tallow have been added. Soft grounds permit a limitless number of textural effects.

Solvent A solution used for cleaning the paint from blocks, metal plates, stones, or silk screens.

Squeegee A device usually made of rubber and with a wooden handle that is used to pull paint across the screen when printing a serigraph.

Stencil A piece of parchment, thin sheet-metal, paper, or the like so perforated that when it is laid on a surface, and paint or ink applied, a desirable image is reproduced.

Stencil brush A short, stiff-bristle brush designed for stencil techniques.

Stencil paper A parchment or wax-coated, stiff paper used in making stencils. It is usually transparent or translucent.

Stop bath A mild acid rinse (about 3 per cent acetic acid) used to stop the action of the developer.

Stop-out A liquid or paste substance which protects those areas of a printing plate that are not to be etched. (*See* Ground.)

Tarlatan A stiff gauze material much like cheesecloth used to wipe the ink from metal plates in intaglio printing.

Telephoto lens (*See* Telescopic lens.)

Telescopic lens A lens which produces a magnified image, designed principally to photograph objects at a distance.

Tusche A liquid substance used in lithography, etching, and serigraphy to prepare those areas which are eventually to be printed.

Undercutting The act of cutting away from the underside of a linoleum or wood block or a metal plate (with acid) so as to leave it without proper support.

Vignette A photograph having a background that is shaded off gradually into the surrounding ground or unprinted paper.

White line A line print in which the image is executed in white line on a dark background.

Woodcut A flat slab or block of wood from which an image has been cut in relief to be printed; also a print from such a block.

Wood engraving A process of printing from a block of end-grain wood which has been engraved with a burin or graver; also a print obtained from such a process.

Xylography The art of printing from wood engravings.

Bibliography

Arnold, Grant, *Creative Lithography and How to Do It.* New York: Harper & Row, Publishers, 1941.

Baranski, Matthew, *Graphic Design.* Scranton, Pennsylvania: International Textbook Company, 1960.

Biegeleisen, J. I., *Silk Screen Stencil Craft as a Hobby.* New York: Harper & Row, Publishers, 1939.

——— and E. J. Busenbark, *The Silk Screen Printing Process,* 2nd ed. New York: McGraw-Hill Book Company, Inc., 1941.

——— and M. A. Cohn, *Silk Screen Stenciling as a Fine Art.* New York: McGraw-Hill Book Company, Inc., 1942.

Bliss, Douglas P., *History of Wood Engraving.* New York: E. P. Dutton & Co., Inc., 1928.

Blum, André, *The Origins of Printing and Engraving.* New York: Charles Scribner's Sons, 1940.

Bowler, Stanley W., *Photography for Boys and Girls.* New York: Thomas Y. Crowell Company, 1952.

Buckland-Wright, John, *Etching and Engraving.* New York: Thomas Y. Crowell Company, 1954.

Craven, Thomas, *Treasury of American Prints.* New York: Simon and Schuster, Inc., 1943.

D'Amico, Victor, *Creative Teaching in Art,* rev. ed. Scranton, Pennsylvania: International Textbook Company, 1953.

Dehn, A. A. and L. L. Barrett, *How to Draw and Print Lithographs.* New York: Tudor Publishing Co., 1950.

Deschin, Jacob, *Say It with Your Camera.* New York: A. S. Barnes & Co., 1960.

Evans, Ralph M., *Eye, Film, and Camera in Color Photography.* New York: John Wiley & Sons, Inc., 1959.

Feininger, Andreas, *Successful Photography.* Englewood Cliffs, New Jersey: Prentice-Hall, Inc., 1954.

Fletcher, F. Morey, *Wood Block Printing.* London: Sir Isaac Pitman & Sons, Ltd., 1935.

Gorbaty, Norman, *Print Making with a Spoon.* New York: Reinhold Publishing Corporation, 1960.

Gottlieb, William P., *Photography with Basic Cameras.* New York: Alfred A. Knopf, Inc., 1953.

Hayter, Stanley W., *New Ways of Gravure.* New York: Pantheon Books, Inc., 1949.

Heller, Jules, *Printmaking Today.* New York: Holt, Rinehart & Winston, Inc., 1958.

Ivins, William M., *How Prints Look.* Boston: Beacon Press, Inc., 1958.

Kafka, Francis J., *Linoleum Block Printing.* New York: Taplinger Publishing Company, Inc., 1958.

Kellsey, Lewis L., *Corrective Photography: An Elementary Illustrated Textbook on Camera Swings and How to Use Them.* Chicago: L. F. Deardorff & Sons, 1947.

Kosloff, Albert, *Screen Process Printing.* Cincinnati, Ohio: Signs of the Times Publishing Co., 1950.

Lumsden, E. S., *The Art of Etching.* New York: Dover Publications, Inc., 1929.

Marshall, Lucile R., *Photography for Teen-Agers,* 2nd ed. Englewood Cliffs, New Jersey: Prentice-Hall, Inc., 1957.

Mayer, Ralph, *The Artist's Handbook of Materials and Techniques,* rev. ed. New York: The Viking Press, Inc., 1957.

McCoy, Robert, *Practical Photography,* rev. ed. New York: Taplinger Publishing Company, Inc., 1960.

McLeish, Minnie, *New Color Cuts.* Peoria, Illinois: Chas. A. Bennett Co., Inc., 1957.

Miller, Thomas and Wyatt Brummett, *This Is Photography: Its Means and Ends.* New York: Doubleday & Co., Inc., 1959.

Morgan, Willard D. and others, *Graphic Graflex Photography,* 11th ed. New York: Morgan and Morgan, Publishers, 1958.

Morrow, B. F., *The Art of Aquatint.* New York: G. P. Putman's Sons, 1935.

Mortensen, William, *Flash in Modern Photography,* 2nd ed. New York: A. S. Barnes & Co., 1947.

Neblette, Carroll Bernard, *Photography: Its Materials and Processes,* 5th ed. New York: D. Van Nostrand Co., Inc., 1952.

Newick, John, *Making Colour Prints: An Approach to Lino Cutting.* Peoria, Illinois: Chas. A. Bennett Co., Inc., 1953.

Peterdi, Gabor, *Printing Methods Old and New.* New York: The Macmillan Company, 1959.

Pyle, Clifford, *Etching Principles and Methods.* New York: Harper & Row, Publishers, 1941.

Ray, Henry W., "Experimental and Creative Photography," *Art Education Bulletin.* Kutztown, Pennsylvania: Eastern Arts Association, XIX, No. 5 (June 1962), 25–33.

Reed, Earl H., *Etching.* New York: G. P. Putnam's Sons, n.d.

Sachs, Paul J., *Modern Prints and Drawings.* New York: Alfred A. Knopf, Inc., 1954.

Scacheri, Mario and M. D. Scacheri, *Fun of Photography.* New York: Harcourt, Brace & World, Inc., 1938.

Schinneller, James, *Art: Search and Self-Discovery.* Scranton, Pennsylvania: International Textbook Company, 1961.

Silsby, Wilson, *Etching Methods and Materials: A New and Simplified Technique.* New York: Dodd, Mead & Co., 1943.

Smith, C., *Experiments in Relief Printmaking.* Charlottesville, Virginia: University of Virginia Press, 1954.

Stephenson, J. B., *From Old Stencils to Silk Screening.* New York: Charles Scribner's Sons, 1953.

Sternberg, Harry, *Modern Methods and Materials of Etching.* New York: McGraw-Hill Book Company, Inc., 1949.

———, *Silk Screen Color Printing.* New York: McGraw-Hill Book Company, Inc., 1942.

Strauss, Victor, "Modern Silk Screen Printing," *Print,* VII (November 1952), 21–36.

Tanner, Robin, *Children's Work in Block Printing.* Leicester, England: Dryad Press, 1936.

Torrey, Frederic, *The Art of Etching.* Berkeley, California: University of California Press, 1923.

Watson, E. and N. Kent, *Relief Print; Woodcut, Wood Engraving & Linoleum Cut.* New York: Watson-Guptill Publications, Inc., 1945.

Wengenroth, Stow, *Making a Lithograph,* How to Do It Series, Vol. XI. New York: The Viking Press, Inc., 1936.

West, Levon, *Making an Etching,* How to Do It Series, Vol. I. New York: The Viking Press, Inc., 1932.

Woolner, H., *Teaching Fabric Printing in Schools.* London: Evans Brothers, Limited, n.d.

Zigrosser, Carl, *Book of Fine Prints,* rev. ed. New York: Crown Publishers, Inc., 1956.

———, *Expressionists.* New York: George Braziller, Inc., 1957.

———, *Six Centuries of Fine Prints.* New York: Doubleday & Co., Inc., 1939.

Index

Index

E

R

S

T

U

V

W

Z